COMMENTS ABOUT P

"The 2008 presidential campaign placed much positive emphasis (by Republicans, at least) on an old word—maverick. Without attempting to define "maverick," I believe Bill Peach is one, in the most positive way, especially given the region and the church in which he was first nurtured.

"Though Bill has never forsaken his roots, rejected longtime friends, nor renounced lifelong associations, he is completely independent and insightful in his thinking, honest and forthright in his linguistic expression, and bold and courageous in his eloquence.

"His thinking and his writing remind me so much of that of Will Campbell, little wonder given Bill's respect for Campbell. Given my own interest in politics, religion, and culture, I never want to miss one of Bill's essays. And while only rarely might I disagree with him, I never fail to be challenged by his writing."

—Perry C. Cotham, Ph.D.
University professor, minister, and author
One World/Many Neighbors

"Bill Peach is a rare soul. He is a conversationalist who becomes vulnerable through his writing. He and I sometimes are on opposite sides of issues, but our love and respect for each other is unwavering. In his writings you will encounter opinion and truth, blended in love. Bill is a rare jewel in our community."

—Rev. Scott Roley, senior pastor
Christ Community Church, Franklin, Tenn.

"I have been fortunate to have read most of the essays compiled in this book. I believe you will find here an unusual understanding of the differences that exist between conservative and liberal religious outlooks. I am not sure I coined it, but I often refer to Bill Peach as 'The Franklin Philosopher.' His thoughts inspired me to arrange to have him preach at my church."

—Charles Sumner, President Emeritus, Nashville Chapter
Americans United for Separation of Church and State

"During the past years of liberal, conservative, and religious extremism, the musings of Bill Peach have provided his readers a refuge of political rationalism."
—Charles H. McNutt, Ph.D., Professor Emeritus
Department of Anthropology, University of Memphis

"Bill Peach listens, asks questions, and learns with an openness that is refreshingly engaging."
—Bob Cowperthwaite, rector
St. Paul's Episcopal Church, Franklin, Tenn.

"Not many can write interestingly and thoughtfully about topics as broad-ranging as politics, preaching, and philosophy, but Bill Peach does just that in these essays. Bill has a gentle humor that allows even those who disagree, to profit from what he writes. It has been my pleasure to read many of these via email. His thoughts were among the emails that I didn't overlook. Now that they are available in print, they certainly should not be overlooked by others."
—Will Berger, co-pastor
Historic Franklin Presbyterian Church, Franklin, Tenn.

"Bill is a levelheaded, wide-ranging thinker with a global perspective. A reader will glean a healthy harvest from his philosophical fomentations. As essayist, he attempts to improve the world one idea at a time."
—Joe Speer, editor
Beatlick News

"Reading Bill Peach's work reminds me of what we all have in common, not how we differ. His thoughts and reflections cause me to seek understanding of how my beliefs fit in the overall scheme. I appreciate this book for its challenging singular thinking."
—Lynn Heady, president
Congregation Micah Synagogue, Brentwood, Tenn.

"*Thoughtful, insightful,* and *well-written* are some of the adjectives that come to mind upon reading Bill Peach's ruminations on religion, politics, and language. Any reader who reads *Politics, Preaching & Philosophy* will gain valuable insights into these topics."

—Saritha Prabhu, columnist
The Nashville *Tennessean*

"These essays exhibit a sense of curiosity that is sometimes mischievous, sometimes strikingly candid, but always fruitful and instructive. They don't care to let sleeping dogs lie, but offer constructive insights that challenge our complacency and partisan interests, regardless as to where our partisan loyalties belong. They give voice to some of the hidden recesses within our thoughts that we might prefer go unspoken, lest we provide support to those with whom we disagree. Heated controversies are treated here with a warm heart, and compassionate countenances are found on those whom we sometimes thought to be ogres and monsters. These essays make clear why thoughtful people can disagree, and why we'll continue to disagree, but they offer the hope that we might do so with a bit less antagonism and suspicion. Bill's gentleness and keenness of thought are much needed and appreciated."

—Steve Hammontree
Department of History, Politics and Philosophy
Lipscomb University
Nashville, Tenn.

"A good writer is really an artist, one who entertains the reader while at the same time moves them toward deeper thought and greater understanding. Bill is one such writer. His has a mastery of words and an uncanny ability to take a complex idea and distill it down to its essence, and take a simple idea and show it's not so simple after all. Prepare to be inspired and entertained at the same time."

—Ginny Welsch
Publisher, *The Nashville Free Press*

"Bill Peach combines intellect and heart in this wonderful and diverse collection of essays. He draws from his rich Southern upbringing to tell stories of his family, church, and community, and uses them to challenge our thinking on a wide range of religious, social, and philosophical questions. You don't always have to agree with Bill on where he comes out, but you will always be challenged to think through your own feelings and positions on issues that we all face in our daily living and in society today. He poses important dilemmas and contradictions in our current ways of thinking and offers freedom from being caught in the past—offering new and more inclusive ways of understanding others and our increasingly small and richly diverse world."

—The Rev. Dr. Dan Rosemergy, minister
Greater Nashville Unitarian Universalist Congregation

Politics, Preaching & Philosophy

To Paul!

Bill Peach
3-20-2011

ALSO BY BILL PEACH

To Think As a Pawn
A play in three acts
1990

The South Side of Boston
A memoir
1995

Random Thoughts Left & Right
A collection of essays, articles, and short fiction
1998

POLITICS, PREACHING & PHILOSOPHY

BILL PEACH

PUBLISHED BY WESTVIEW, INC.,
NASHVILLE, TENNESSEE

Politics, Preaching & Philosophy
by Bill Peach

Copyright © 2009 by Bill Peach
2009 Published by Westview, Inc.,
Nashville, Tennessee

All rights reserved.

Cover concept *Dea Peach-Carmon*
Cover layout *Paula Underwood Winters*
Text layout *Renee Butler*

Set in Book Antiqua and Trajan

Many of these essays may be accessed at
www.williamsonherald.com, search Bill Peach.
No part of this book may be reproduced or copied in any
form without the written permission of Bill Peach.

ISBN: 978-1-935271-07-9

Printed in the United States of America

To five generations of love

Mammy

Mother

Emily

Becca, Lucie, and Dea

Addison, Shelby, Emmy, Brant, Maddie, Ford, and Athena

Table of Contents

    Acknowledgments xii

    Foreword xv

1. Political Correctness 1
2. A Different Kind of Courage for Compassion. 4
3. Secular Ethics and Religious Ethics 7
4. Intellectuals and Academics 10
5. The Church Next Door 13
6. The Willing and the Unwilling 16
7. Dressing for Civility. 19
8. Defining Democracy in Two Words. 22
9. On Being, or Not Being, from Around Here 25
10. The Dogmatic Uncertainty of Knowing and Believing . . 28
11. The Line Between Heritage and Hatred 31
12. The Nouns and Adjectives of Extremism 34
13. Finding Peace in the War on Christmas 37
14. Thinking and Praying Out Loud. 40
15. English: Our Language of Choice and Necessity 43
16. Ripples of Blue in a Puddle of Red 46
17. Bang the Drum Softly 49
18. Education: Our Right or Responsibility 52
19. On Innocence and Humility 55
20. Retail: A Profession, or Product, or Price 58
21. The Blind Men and the Elephant 61
22. On the Fairness Doctrine 64
23. The Philosophy of Antitheses. 67
24. Judging One's Cover by a Book 70
25. On Being Religiously Literate. 73

Table of Contents

26. One Nation, Divisible 76
27. Divine Intervention 79
28. The Reasonable Rhetoric of the Road 82
29. Article VI, No Religious Test 85
30. The Best of Times, the Worst of Times 88
31. Ideologues, Idealists, and Idiots 91
32. Wall of Separation 94
33. The Mind and Soul of America 97
34. The Fallacy of Fear 100
35. The Un-Churched and the Over-Churched 103
36. The Naked Lapel 106
37. Misspeaking and Misthinking 109
38. Ego, Elitism, and Excellence 112
39. ROTC, Recruiters, and Resisters 115
40. Liberation Theology 118
41. Controversy, Consensus, and Compromise 121
42. The Unlikely Resolution of Life and Choice 124
43. The First and Second Amendments 127
44. The Age of Evangelical Enlightenment 130
45. A Generation of Philosophers 133
46. Tambourine Theology 136
47. The Corruption of Children 139
48. The Handiwork of God 142
49. God's Will, Sunday Morning 145
50. Pastors, Preachers, and Philosophers 148
51. The God of Politics 151
52. Tolerance, Condescension, and Understanding 154

Acknowledgments

Mindy Tate, editor of the *Williamson Herald*, was kind to honor my request to submit the series of essays that became this book. The first essay ran on May 7, 2006. She gave me no restraint in content or bias and gave me the challenge to compose my thoughts in a concise journalistic style.

I owe much of my writing ambition to The Council for the Written Word, which, as an organization and group of individuals who love the written word, continues to educate, encourage, and empower local writers. They were kind to include me in the CWW Hall of Fame in 2001.

My introduction to writing came at the invitation of the Pull-Tight Players, who performed my one-act play in 1971, which became the opening act for my first book.

I have to thank the editors and publishers with whom I have worked on earlier publications: John, Myra, and Mark Ishee of JM Productions; Mary Bray Wheeler and Andy Miller of Providence House Publishers; and Roger Waynick of Cool Springs Press and publisher of the *Our Voices* anthologies, which gave voice to 72 local writers.

Much appreciation is due to the staff of Humanities Tennessee who have made me feel a part of the Southern literary community as forum participant and session host.

I have been blessed to have around my email roundtable a dozen or more dedicated teachers of English who have embraced me and moved my commas and semicolons into their proper places with gently corrective kindness.

I am grateful to those in the political, spiritual, and academic communities who have encouraged me when they believed my thoughts were positive and benign. Also, I thank those of the religious and political right in Williamson, who honed my language and softened my temperament in moments of disagreement and confrontation.

The final refinement of this work is the handiwork of Kathryn Knight. Her editorial skills gave a literate seamlessness to my random thoughts.

Politics, Preaching & Philosophy

Foreword

In a community long known for its affluence, its religious conservatism, and its overwhelmingly Republican political convictions, Bill Peach is an arresting anomaly. A native son, a main-street businessman and mainstream Christian, an Army Reserve veteran, a longtime dues-paying member of the Rotary Club and the Chamber of Commerce, he is also a self-confessed Liberal known for his plain-spoken minority views—against the war in Iraq and executions at the state penitentiary, for individual freedom of choice regarding abortion, and our collective obligation in the funding of public education.

Every town worth its salt needs a Bill Peach—needs lots of them. Always thoughtful, usually soft-spoken, he is never afraid to speak with a different voice, one seldom heard among the many voices of Williamson County. Instead of going off half-cocked when misguided notions are widely perceived to be eternal verities, he thinks deeply and commits his thoughts to paper—and more often than not, his carefully considered perspectives turn out to be correct. Not popular, perhaps, but simply right.

Bill Peach's short, pithy commentaries, collected here as random thoughts, are his way of serving the sometimes-wayward community to which he has devoted a lifetime of affection. Tough love, you might call it—the kind that can give courage and strength to one person or an entire town.

John Egerton
Journalist, author, editor
December 17, 2008

1

Political Correctness

Political correctness is a term used to describe language that we have devised to inflict the least possible offense to any designated group. Many conservative politicians, activists, and journalists insist there is an organized liberal political-correctness movement designed to promote multiculturalism, feminism, gender neutrality, secularism, and other forms of social engineering. Most Liberals deny the existence of political correctness and see such references as distractions from any substantive debate on changes in our language to more accurately depict our culture.

Consequently, political correctness is not politically correct, and that which was intended to provide a minimum of offense has become offensive to everyone. The harder we have tried to get our language right, the more we have blurred the lines between ambiguity and reality and between inclusion and exclusion.

When and how did we get it wrong? In our benign attempt to cleanse our language of intolerance and ridicule, we have formed new words to identify any and all who are impaired, challenged, or in any way different from ourselves in learning ability, physical stature and agility, color of skin, hair, or eyes, geographic origin, gender, sexual orientation, and other human attributes derived at birth or fortune from a benevolent and indiscriminate God.

How did we come to designate women as a minority? Why is a child with six generations of ancestors in Middle Tennessee referred to as African-American, or my children called Anglo or European? Are we not all now American and all gifted in some way and uniquely special in our individual needs?

We have also added a language of universality and separation in matters of faith. We have sent our apostles out at daybreak and the eleventh hour to bring whosoever would come to God. Saint and sinner, rich and poor, pinstripes and denim fill the pews of ubiquitous and monolithic assemblies under a banner that reads *nondenominational*. With a strong and certain message of tolerance and denial, we avow to all that we are neither Baptist nor Methodist, neither Catholic, Protestant, nor Jew.

We have added the designation *progressive* to break out of the stigma of being a Liberal, and added *compassionate* to escape the image of the self-serving Conservative. We have found it necessary to display our national flag in houses of worship and erect crosses and display ecclesiastical dictates on the halls of government. In fear of offending with our holiday greetings, we deny ourselves our own freedom of expression and, at the same time, treat with contempt the stranger who calls his God by a different name and whose days of worship we do not observe.

We have added euphemisms and misnomers to temper the excesses of behavior and politics. We have obscured the finality of death in the arms of a loving God. We have obscured the violence of war in technological description and pride of ownership of intelligent weaponry. We feel it necessary to apologize for our successes and our blessings and to rationalize for our failures and our shortcomings. We have ineptly applied the labels of freedom, patriotism, family or traditional values, liberal, and Christian to include the behavior and voices of those who bring dishonor and deception to the purity of our institutions.

Political correctness usually seems to apply to the language and philosophy of least resistance, the collective and historical voice of the majority. It has also come to imply a language of accommodation within which we are forced to give away our inalienable rights to an undeserving, over-sensitive minority.

Anytime we try to avoid political correctness, our language will surely become politically incorrect. Depending on where we live and the political majority of the citizenry, we can still find some pleasure and satisfaction in incorrectness of language, as long as we watch our spelling and punctuation, and speak or write with a voice that shows no trace of anger or intolerance.

2

A Different Kind of Courage for Compassion

The now-forgotten trial and conviction of 9/11 terrorist Zacarias Moussaoui was an emotional development in the war on terror. Whether or not it ended with a fair and just decision rendered by a courageous and deliberative jury is still being debated. Those of us who live in the South may not easily identify with the opinions expressed by the jury or the survivors of the World Trade Center victims. Living in the Bible Belt, in a county with a church on every corner, we have come to accept the religious tradition and the writings of Thomas Aquinas that sustain the belief that the death penalty is necessary to deter acts of violence and maintain order in society.

This horrific crime, which contributed to or enabled the tragedy of 9/11 and the deaths of 3000 people, met or even exceeded the court's legal justification for capital punishment. The jury struggled for seven days before deciding on a verdict of life in prison. Public officials, politicians, and religious leaders have been hesitant to condemn or praise the decision, but seem to feel that our system of justice has prevailed, and they have not voiced great disappointment.

Some found finality in believing that life in prison without parole for a suicidal religious fanatic may be a more cruel punishment than death. The jury denied him his martyrdom and condemned him to obscurity in an isolated cubicle in Colorado. Life in prison may have satisfied the primal and religious public demand for justice and vengeance.

In the aftermath of the acts of barbarity of 2001, we embraced the families of the victims and reacted with sadness and moral outrage, and lashed out at religious fanatics and nations and governments and enemies real and imagined who played any part in this assault. What was unique about this trial was the demeanor and attitude of the families of the victims. Twelve members of those families testified for the defense. In spite of their sadness and their anger, their words of reason and compassion give us hope. The rules of the trial forbade their telling the jury that they favored life over death, but their intent was clear. Robin Theurkauf, a victim family member and divinity student at Yale, said, "We may have given [the jurors] permission to free themselves from an obligation to respond to the massive grief with vengeance. We allowed them to view the case dispassionately."

Patricia Perry, whose son died at the World Trade Center, said, "Beyond the verdict in this trial, I oppose using the death penalty to demonstrate to citizens that murder is so wrong, that we will kill to prove it wrong. State killing teaches our children that we do not mean what we say and inures us as a society to the horror of killing."

Loretta Filipov, whose husband was in the plane that hit the first tower, said, "Killing Zacarias Moussaoui will not bring my husband back. It will not change the life my family and I now have without my husband and their father. But what killing will do is to continue the cycle of violence, hate, and revenge. This is not the face we want for our future, for our children and grandchildren."

These are probably not words that you normally hear on Sunday morning at your steeple of choice. These are probably not words that you hear at Starbuck's or the local meat-and-three, or at Rotary or chamber of commerce lunches. Some may even see this verdict as a sign of weakness. It has been challenged by some religious and political writers. For me, I think I saw in these families and this jury a better image of our system of justice and our religion. Compassion requires a different kind of courage.

3

Secular Ethics and Religious Ethics

In a classroom at Lipscomb University, the writer of the textbook raised the question of comparing secular ethics with religious ethics. The course was Ethical Theory, and I took it in 1998 in my fifth decade as a college student. It was my first formal philosophy course, though most of my fun reading had been either from philosophy, theology, or political science.

It was a bit ironic that my only course in philosophy would be taught by a Church of Christ preacher in a Church of Christ affiliated university. In the discussion, I offered the proposition that secular ethics are stronger than religious ethics, in that religious ethics are driven by specific divine commands and prohibitions and tend to promote minimalism and mediocrity in today's pulpit culture.

The instructor, whose name I will not disclose, to protect his Lipscomb image, responded with a cough and throat-clearing, which I interpreted as a prelude to refutation. As an apology, I suggested that I had offered the idea for shock value, knowing he would disagree with me. To my surprise, he admitted that he agreed. I have since wondered how two reasonably intelligent Church of Christ scholars could have come to this commonality of the mind, when most church-goers see secular and ethics as contradictory terminology.

In that course, we studied several ethical theories—deontological, teleological, aretaic, and religious-text based, conveying the commands of a deity. These are ethics based on duty, benefit, conscience, virtue, divine command, and combinations thereof.

My earliest experience with religion was with a fundamentalist authoritarian dogma of requisites for salvation and accompanying warnings of moral violations that determined where we would spend post-mortal eternity. These principles continue to be the underpinnings of most major religious bodies.

Additionally, and more importantly, churches and churchgoers in the South are on the front lines with food, clothing, and shelter in the aftermath of tornado, flood, fire, and famine. They are the providers of love at the bedside and graveside. They bring the best in Southern cooking to the funeral home and assisted living facility, and feed the hunger of grief and loneliness. This is religion at its best.

As Southern culture changed, mainstream Southern fundamental churches began to lose members in two directions, almost in opposite directions. Several decades ago, traditional Christianity lost some of its membership over a perception of moral inconsistency in questions of racial equality and nonviolence. Fundamentalism was seen as being more doctrinal and heaven-centered, but having little influence on the human condition, ethical behavior, or intellectual integrity.

Some of us looked for spiritual peace in liberal churches. Some of us found greater spiritual enrichment outside the walls of organized religion. We went out in search of a religion of intellect and social activism. We found pleasure in random acts of kindness and the philosophical reformation of Southern culture, but there was an emptiness in our not having the skill to bake and deliver the Christian covered dish.

Many of us are still somewhere between the church of our youth and the church we have spent our lives trying to find. We watch in awe and are clueless about the prophetic certainty and charismatic appeal of a new Christianity that we do not feel or understand. We see giant auditoriums with full orchestras and rock bands and rap groups, and wonder why we do not feel driven to dance or laugh or raise our arms or voices in praise.

We still believe that the ethical admonitions of Jesus are the same basic truths that effect the greatest good in human behavior. If there is a valid comparison between secular ethics and religious ethics, it may have been that I was hearing it in a classroom setting of reason and logic. It just seemed clearer and maybe more secular without the drums and the bass guitars.

4

Intellectuals and Academics

Occasionally, when I am trying to provoke a discussion, I suggest that Williamson County is academic but not intellectual. I get various responses. Those who agree usually nod and smile as if they truly believe there is a difference. This would include many who believe that *intellectual* has a qualitative advantage over what they perceive to be an education of expedience and necessity, some of whom actually prefer an education of contemplative arts over pragmatic arts.

There are others who would advise—in a variation of a Willie Nelson warning—Mamas, don't let your babies grow up to be intellectuals. Those who assign more value to the pragmatic arts may equate intellectuals with liberal New England universities rather than the academies of ancient Greece. Our political history is strewn with skeletons of unsuccessful candidates for public office who could neither escape the randomness nor define the certainty of their book learning.

The majority of our locals most frequently view the two words as interchangeable—a single valid instrument by which we measure the academic excellence of our student population and a quality of life within an area with minimal similarity to a less-literate culture depicted in earlier Southern literature. We use either word to identify excellence as opposed to mediocrity or deficiency. We imply both the mastery of a body of information and the intellectual inquiry into its meaning. There is in America a populist movement against intellectual elitism, which, in an environment of political fear, can inhibit progressive academic pursuits. Sincere efforts to stifle intellectual curiosity can also impede the growth of academic skills.

There is also a concurrent movement in America that is reshaping our religious configuration. The numerical growth in church attendance and religious involvement has been greater in denominations that promote theological determinism rather than human or natural influences in current events. This contributes to a perceived rift between those who find spiritual certainty from the pages of Scripture, and rationalists who find divine wisdom in a presence beyond the reach of human interpretation.

There is also a divide between historians and philosophers. The line is obscure, in that the difference lies in emphasis and priority. With some exceptions, historians see human destiny shaped by war and the cause and aftermath thereof. In contrast, philosophers divide history into chronological and cyclical transitions of human thought. Williamson County, with its rich heritage of historical literature, archival documentation, architectural preservation, and strong reverence for its land and ancestry, is blessed with historians, some of whom are also excellent philosophers. But, our monuments and our written words portray the valor of battle more often than other events of lesser conflict.

Some would suggest that Republicans tend to be academic and Democrats tend to be intellectual. This depends on your definitions. Historically, citizens at the top and bottom of the intelligence scale have been attracted to liberalism, communism, anarchy and the Democratic Party. Those of average and slightly above intelligence have populated the ranks of conservatism, despotism, and the Republican Party. At least, we have heard this to defend or castigate historical identities and public servants.

Williamson County schools have the highest test scores in Tennessee. Williamson County is approximately 73% Republican. Those who would suggest that Republicans are not education-friendly should look at Williamson County and the nonpartisan support of education. The misconception may be attributed to the public image of President Bush. While the President may have done a disservice to the repute of an MBA, his ineptitude was more in his clumsiness of language and logic than in his level of academic achievement.

I would not try to define intellectuals and academics along well-defined lines. You can offer many comparisons and contrasts between Evangelicals and Episcopalians, Democrats and Republicans, Liberals and Conservatives, but you will find academics and intellectuals in all groups. Whether you believe there is a difference could be the result, or maybe the cause of, your preference for inclusion, or exclusion.

5

THE CHURCH NEXT DOOR

Those of us who grew up in a rural South spent some of our best of times in a one-room country church. The church in Boston (Tennessee) sits on land donated by our family. Three generations led singing, baked communion bread, fed preachers, mowed grass, swept floors, and tended to God's house with loving care. Just down the road at the corner of Garrison Road and Peach Hollow sits a small Methodist church with roots in the preaching of my great-grandfather, William Strickland Peach.

Even after I came to Franklin, I found spiritual comfort in a historical building that I shared with 400 other Christians who were also friends and neighbors. I read the words of Jesus telling Peter that he would build a Church. I knew he wasn't talking about brick and mortar, but I think he would have been comfortable in the pews at Fourth Avenue, as I knew he had been at Boston.

Who could have thought that after 2000 years of church history, Congress would pass a piece of legislation that we call the Religious Land Use and Institutionalized Persons Act? Who could have foreseen the prolific litigation over establishment and free exercise of religion? Who could imagine Christians leaving the church of their ancestors and renting space in a school after a property takeover by a new eldership? Who could have predicted that a group of 18 homeowners would file legal action to prevent the building of a 41,000-square-foot Bethel World Outreach building in their neighborhood?

About half of us believe that America, including conservative Williamson County, is becoming secular and humanistic, and that the ACLU is trying to eliminate God from the public forum. The other half of us believe that America is in danger of becoming a theocracy. We fear an administration that governs at the will of a conservative religious voter base. We find both celebration and gnashing of teeth over the religious McCarthyism of the Fifties and the activist Supreme Court decisions of the Sixties.

Those of us who sit on elected or appointed boards struggle with these coexisting, conflicting views. Our religious heritage commits us to defend the free exercise of religion and to protect the rights of all, secular and religious. We bring to public office our church affiliations and our interpretation of the Constitution, but we are often subjected to intimidation by those who seek preferential treatment, pleading a divine presence on one side of the scales of civil justice.

We often hear the acronym NIMBY—Not In My Back Yard. Recently, I heard someone refer to BANANA—Build Absolutely Nothing Anywhere Near Anything. Even the newest resident who moved into our county last week would like to burn the bridge, or build a wall, or dig a moat to secure our borders and stop the immigration of out-of-county aliens. With each new residential development comes the need for a school, a church, a shopping center, and two new turn lanes at every new traffic light.

In Boston, the two-room school and the one-room church sat on the same property, half a mile from our house. In Boston, half a mile meant next door. A country store was just over a small bridge crossing a shallow creek that flowed beside the church and school. The school closed in 1956. The church and store remain, the historical heartbeat of a body of believers and a handful of new friends from somewhere else.

Our Founding Fathers carefully crafted the First Amendment to guarantee religious freedom for individuals and to prohibit government from giving unfair advantage to the sectarian over the secular. A church building, like any other structure, is an earthly edifice, not a spiritual entity. When it has 41,000 square feet and is open for business seven days a week, and encroaches on the residential serenity of homeowners, it becomes a Wal-Mart with a steeple.

6

THE WILLING AND THE UNWILLING

We watched for the mail carrier's car every day for a letter from Uncle Allen who was serving across Western Europe in World War II. Mammy, my grandmother, agonized over the killing and the dying. Granddaddy worried more about the dying. He said the killing was just a part of war.

Two young soldiers that we all knew were killed early in the war. A cousin was hit by a piece of shrapnel and was left with limited use of an arm. Young men who were not called for the draft felt the unspoken envy of military families, and volunteered for the Army or Navy. There was no refuge from the war.

I understood the deep anger of World War II veterans as they watched my generation burn flags, shout obscenities, march and carry signs, and question the moral integrity of our President and our secretaries of state and defense. The greatest generation watched the news at six and ten and tried to make sense of My Lai and Kent State while their sons and younger brothers were being shipped home in body bags.

For me, joining the Army Reserve was a moral compromise between being a draft-dodger and a draft-evader. After active duty or a weekend Reserve meeting, I couldn't wait to get out of my olive-drab fatigues and back into a civilian coat and tie.

Bill Peach

I wondered if the older people were looking at my uniform and remembering a husband or son killed in France or the Pacific. How could I have told them that this war was a mistake and I was not brave and was not going to die defending freedom, or America, or God, or whatever their husbands and sons had died for? My conversations and confrontations with college and high school students left mixed impressions of my being either an unpatriotic, anti-war, draft-dodging hippie, or someone who burned huts and killed babies in Vietnam.

The horrible conduct of the American people during and following Vietnam was shameful on both sides. We treated the returning soldiers and campus protesters with hostility and open displays of contempt. I was part of the anger and also a target of that anger. I am proud to have worn a uniform that I had never wanted to put on for six years. I pledge allegiance to my country and my flag with the heart and soul of a veteran and an aging flower-child. I am honored to stand when veterans are being recognized, but feel unworthy to share applause with combat heroes.

I voted against Richard Nixon, and found comfort in his resignation. I questioned the logic and conduct of a war, and did so because I loved my country and my brothers-in-arms.

A relevant question arose recently when one congregation of the United Methodist Church offered sanctuary to military resistors who refused deployment to Iraq. Members of the media were quick to remind us that these men and women took an oath to serve and did so willingly. Does it make a difference when the military is all-volunteer rather than conscripted? Do the same rules apply to the willing and the unwilling? Can a young soldier or marine ever say, "This war is a mistake and I am not brave and I am not going to die in Iraq for freedom, or America, or God, or whatever they are dying for"?

Our letters from Uncle Allen continued until the end of the war in Europe. He came home to loving parents and family and an admiring nation. He was greeted with parades and hugs and kisses, and never questioned the rightness of the war nor doubted the necessity of his service.

I often attribute to Mammy my reason for being a Liberal. She loved her God and her country and her only son, and dutifully accepted the thought of his dying. She just never spoke any good feelings about the war or the killing.

7

Dressing for Civility

Two of the books recently in the top five on the *New York Times* Best Seller list were John Dean's *Conservatives Without Conscience* and Ann Coulter's *Godless: The Church of Liberalism*. I have not read either, but the titles are reflections of our inflammatory reciprocal monologue that has promoted incivility of human interaction. Conservatives tend to trace the decline of behavior in America to the tie-dyed, bell-bottomed upheaval of the Sixties with its drugs, sex, and disrespect for patriotism and religion. The Liberals' explanation of the decline is one of ambiguity spanning the last three decades of moral misdirection in politics, religion, the military, and corporate capitalism. I have avoided trying to assign blame. I prefer looking at indicators and trends.

My earliest insight into the ominous change in taste and decorum came within my profession as a men's clothier. Most noticeably in the decade of the Eighties, business and religious leadership infused the not-so-revolutionary idea of casual attire, or business casual, as it was called at the office. The intention was noble. It was to promote a relaxed, egalitarian relationship between CEOs and corporate underlings. Churches, using a similar logic, turned away from a dress code of ties and starched pinpoint oxford shirts with exact neck size and sleeve length under a dark, conservative suit or navy blazer.

Apparel is only one of many art forms, along with music, literature, theater, film, architecture, and other creative expressions, by which we trace and depict the aesthetic cycles of any culture. In fairness, we in the clothing industry see attention to sartorial detail only as an indicator, not in any way as a cause of behavioral variations.

There are many theories about the correlation between dress and behavior. People tend to dress to express a personal interpretation of who they are or hope to become. People also make value judgments about others based on their own rigid standards of dress. These attitudes may be prejudicial or may be rational deductive conclusions based on observations of behavior that are associated with others in similar uniforms of conformity, defiance, hubris, or benign neglect.

The defining moment for me came from a customer who, in explaining his change in buying habits, told me that "we" did not have to wear good clothes anymore. I wondered, but didn't ask, if he had to read good books, or eat good food, or watch good television, or drive a good car.

Public opinion, in official polls and casual conversation, overwhelmingly holds that ethical and moral behavior have declined during whatever period is in question. Some people believe that a downward movement is the unavoidable fate in the cultural trajectory of any nation, culture, religion, or empire. This conclusion cannot be drawn by making limited judgments based on shorter periods of decades or election cycles. I would not suggest that a three-decade decline in taste and appropriateness of apparel presages the fall of the American Empire.

Should we, like British prep-school children, or corporate board rooms, or military units, all wear the same uniform and look and think alike? God and logic forbid. Should we as retailers, corporations, churches, schools, or families establish minimum (or maximum) standards of dress? Does the promotion of Casual Friday or Casual Sunday translate into casual attitudes toward productivity, performance, and behavior?

On the subject of civility, some exciting things are happening in our public schools. Through two or three different programs we are teaching character. Not sectarian dogma, but moral values. We emphasize caring, courage, citizenship, cooperation, fairness, perseverance, respect, responsibility, trustworthiness, and random acts of kindness and compassion. On a similar note, one of my grandsons found some pleasure in selecting a blue-stripe tie to be part of game-day dress for his high school hockey team. This may not be a trend that will save democracy, Christianity, or traditional Southern gentility, but it may be an indicator of better times.

8

DEFINING DEMOCRACY IN TWO WORDS

Political discourse in America has been reduced to the fewest possible words and syllables. Those who hold left-of-center positions in most areas of social and political philosophy thought they had reached an unprecedented depth of superficiality when they truncated the conservative political agenda to the phrase: God, Guns, and Gays. Who could have foreseen the ubiquitous display of a single letter of the alphabet that would reconfigure forever the image of America in the world community?

Imagine our Founding Fathers sweating and toiling over the Preamble, trying to define the complexity of democracy in one simple sentence. From them we have the treasures "more perfect Union," "general Welfare," "domestic Tranquillity," and "common defence," as well as "We hold these truths to be self-evident," not to mention "Life, Liberty and the pursuit of Happiness." English majors may suggest that they should have written more *nearly* perfect union, but we know it is a work in progress.

Our Constitution was written in a time when literacy was cherished by all. The speeches and letters of the Founding Fathers contained poetic and intellectual verbiage beyond the language skills of current shapers of government. Today our political debates have been reduced to bumper stickers and hot-button issues of not more than three words.

My favorite is probably the words *family values*. This is the one campaign statement that is totally meaningless. It has as many definitions as there are families, with differing opinions among family members.

Liberals and Moderates often find offense in the use of phrases whose connotations change depending on the issues being discussed (*e.g.*, traditional marriage, sanctity of life, flag desecration, religious freedom, freedom of choice). Politicians often take the moral high ground by displaying and repeating things that we all believe in (*e.g.*, God Bless America, Support Our Troops, Prayer in Schools).

One day I had a thought while reading a piece of campaign literature from a candidate for the state senate. There is an emotional magic about the Second Amendment. Somehow American gun-owners have become convinced that someone is going to take their guns away. So, I wonder, could Liberals evoke a similar fear regarding the First Amendment? They wouldn't have to explain it, just create some fear that someone was going to take away those rights that were guaranteed in the First Amendment. No candidate or political party has had the foresight or courage to try this.

It is difficult to instill fear through logical discourse. I do not wish for any cataclysmic event to attract voters to the First Amendment. If we were told that someone from the government was coming to our houses to take all of our religious literature, including our Bibles, we would be enraged. On the other hand, if the government passed a law that we all had to read the Bible and recite specific verses on command, we would feel equally threatened. Suppose we were told that during a period of national crisis, we could only speak good things about America and could not condemn or speak evil of the government or its actions lest we give aid and comfort to some real or imagined enemy. Suppose the same applied to news media. Newspapers or broadcast networks that were critical of elected officials might be censured or taken to court. The right to peaceably assemble for redress of grievance might be suspect if the gathering was in protest of some war-related issue or matter of domestic security.

I don't think any political group will jump on this idea between now and the next election. Americans are not yet concerned about the possibility of losing the rights guaranteed in the First Amendment. However, either party with a few million First Amendment bumper stickers, and targeted talk radio, and high-profile Sunday morning sermons could convince the populace that the threat is imminent. Then anyone who did not have a First Amendment bumper sticker on his or her car could easily be identified as someone who opposed the First Amendment.

9

On Being, or Not Being, from Around Here

I was quoted in a newspaper as having said that I was tired of hearing people say they were successful in spite of where they came from, and that my success was *because* of where I came from. Williamson County is more than a nostalgic fascination for historic homes, churches, and former school buildings. Living here instills an emotional and academic reverence for people, place, and time.

Recently, I attended a newsworthy gathering for the Tennessee governor in Leiper's Fork. The crowd included many local elected officials, plus notable poets, pickers, and professionals representing the best of the business, political, and artistic character of this place we love. Thank you, Aubrey Preston (Green's Grocery) and Andy Marshal (Puckett's Grocery), for preserving and respecting the landmarks and rural integrity of my childhood playground.

I attended a similar event at The Factory at Franklin and shared a pleasant morning with several hundred local dignitaries and common folk, including Factory owner Calvin Lehew. Thank you, Calvin, for your vision for Carter's Court, Historic Downtown Franklin, and The Factory, and for your lifetime of commercial and aesthetic contributions to our birthplace.

Politics, Preaching & Philosophy

Then there is Rick Warwick, who came to Williamson County to teach history at Leiper's Fork back when we called it Hillsboro. Exceeded only by Virginia Bowman, Rick has rekindled a reverence for the past far beyond any classroom. Local writer and historian Robert Hicks took Franklin to the book-lovers of Europe with *The Widow of the South*, his masterpiece about a Confederate widow. Add to this list our country-music neighbors who have found a sense of place in the peaceful countryside of Williamson County, away from the gaudy glitter and redneck t-shirts of Music City.

One of my favorite quotes is from a friend who said she was not born in Williamson County, but came as soon as she heard about it. Actually, her family had moved here when she was two years old.

At a time when the local image of religion is being depicted as migratory evangelists, entertainers, and entrepreneurs importing a gospel of charismatic euphoria and numerical evangelism, our faith is restored when we read that Rev. Scott Roley and a crew of God's carpenters are building a home for someone in a place we call Hard Bargain.

Every once in a while you will hear someone remark, "You're not from around here, are you?" We say this without malice or ridicule. This exclusionary designation is a residual of our scars from an attitude long held by those who questioned the right of entry by any means other than local lineage. It was the inevitable introduction for those of us with telltale tan lines who had left the hayfield to come to Franklin to work in retail or at the factory. Today it is directed toward people who run corporations or design and build cars, and developers who purchase farmland and battlefields and cover those hayfields with concrete, brick, and asphalt.

Some longtime residents believe that Downtown Franklin has been taken over by new people. They talk about having bought groceries, hardware, and back-to-school supplies from stores that have closed. They lament not knowing anybody anymore. Many see Main Street as mostly coffee and chocolate and ice cream, and no longer the countywide Saturday destination for replacing the household essentials that sustained a kinder and gentler lifestyle.

With difference in age being one variable, some new people believe that Downtown Franklin existed for hundreds of years with no signs of intelligent life or sophistication—no designer-label boutiques, no wine tasting, no creatively complex coffees—before it became a fun place to hang out and meet friends.

In former times, "being from around here" was measured in generations and Confederate ancestry. Today it doesn't matter where you were born or when you got here. Eventually, some stranger will walk up to you on the street and ask you a simple question, and you will hear a tiny inner voice with sympathy and compassion saying, "You're not from around here, are you?"

10

THE DOGMATIC UNCERTAINTY OF KNOWING AND BELIEVING

Those of us who grew up in fundamentalist churches remember an oft-repeated reference to the wisdom of God and the foolishness of man. There was an implication of a completeness in the body of truth as revealed in Holy Scripture and some inexplicable fear that a secular education would in some way result in some disharmony of faith and intellect.

In my autobiographical memoir, *The South Side of Boson*, an inquisitive eight-year-old struggles with the complexity and simplicity of Southern wisdom. His world consists of a one-room school, a church, a country store, and a three-room home. He believes that school is about knowing, and that church is about believing. If you learn something different at church, you just have to change your believing. However, if you learn something different at school, you have to change your knowing. He listens to adult kinfolk and neighbors who feel little tolerance for revisionist religion or secular scholarship.

He knows, without question, that there are nine planets in our solar system, including a distant and lifeless celestial body called Pluto. The configuration of his solar system fits neatly with his knowledge of nouns and verbs, of addition and subtraction, and the blue, green, and brown markings of a spherical globe. School is about knowing.

As he grows older, not necessarily wiser, he struggles to find harmony in faith and reason, in knowing and believing. He learns that secular wisdom in the halls of academia changes through experimentation, reflection, revision, discovery, and the affirmation or rejection by successive generations of scholarship. In matters of science, history, geography, and informational technology, certainty is limited to currently-accepted knowledge and consensus of interpretation.

Concurrent with this elusive factual uncertainty, he finds a propensity in Southern religion to solidify his cherished beliefs into an intolerant dogma of cultural conformity. Some of his ancestors who led the Restoration Movement and preached the Gospel of Jesus had been unabashed practitioners of involuntary servitude. He has grown up in a segregated South that mandated not only separate drinking fountains and schools, but a separation within the house of God.

He learns in church, and in a male-dominated forum of farmers in a country store, that in a traditional marriage a man is the head of the household and a woman has her place. He finds something incongruent in the pain and frequency of childbirth and the male fascination for primal pleasure long before he will see the political and economic anomalies.

He watches his grandfather physically strike a drunk neighbor who had *cussed* him, and wonders at the tears of his grandmother who had never completely accepted the violent image of Southern masculinity. It is an uneasy conflict that clouds his understanding of the history of man's attraction and resistance to violence. At some point he comes to know, or believe, that survival of self and civility requires a brief and pragmatic departure from the teaching of turning the other cheek and loving your enemies.

The certainty of fundamentalism has historically been an impediment to enlightenment and tolerance. Under a banner of Biblical Truth, we preach an anachronistic and illogically biased interpretation of the role of God in the politics of nationalism. We have discouraged scientific inquiry, fearing its incursion into the fragile faith of literalism. We have questioned membership in the family of God and country over doctrine and ritual.

Even now, I still defer to the wisdom of my grandmother. She said that you should learn everything. It just helps you understand what God has already told you in the Bible. You should know everything, but you don't have to believe everything you know.

Her fascination for books far exceeded her ownership and access to them. Her wisdom was shaped more by instinct and conscience. I don't remember her teaching me much about what she knew. She taught me more about what she believed, which is most of what I know with any certainty today.

11

The Line Between Heritage and Hatred

Within the folklore of Southern mythology are many stories of grandmothers or other genteel maternal figures who drove off bands of Yankee soldiers who were pillaging for food in henhouses and smokehouses. Usually her weapon of defiance was a broom. I grew up with visions of Union soldiers riding away laughing and making plans to return under cover of night, unwilling to fire upon a fragile and poorly equipped Confederate Broom Brigade. One would believe that if these legends were true, we could have, with more old women with brooms, won the war.

Having grown up in southern Williamson County, I still use the first-person pronoun when I identify with the War. My ancestors referred to the conflict as the Civil War. In school, it was often called the War Between the States, which more accurately identified the politics without any implied civility of conduct. When I moved from the country to Franklin, I began to hear about the War (pronounced with two syllables) of Northern Aggression.

In my lifetime we have added three generations of separation from the five tragic hours of the Battle of Franklin in November of 1864. Time should not and does not diminish our reverence for the brave men and boys who died defending their homeland.

In the 40-plus years since the 100th-year commemoration, I have observed many changes. Most importantly, I have watched the regional animosities almost vanish. I have walked through the Confederate Cemetery with friends from Pennsylvania and Illinois. I have stood on the porch of the Carnton mansion and among the cannons on the city square with friends from Michigan and New York. I have come to realize that we are outnumbered today more than we were in 1864. As long as they see their role as one of liberation and not one of occupation, I have no insurgent feelings toward Yankees.

The good news is that we are now a people with a healthy reverence for history and academia. We can now without regional and racial animosity reenact our battles and traditions. We can dress in uniforms of blue and gray and march under battle flags of period authenticity. Those of us who do not share the fascination for military reenactments still support the dramatic depiction of the antebellum heritage of the South and its role in American history. We can restore the palatial plantations and slave quarters and teach the lessons of architecture and agriculture to our children, and still speak openly and academically about an economic system that tolerated and was built upon our ancestral shame of slavery.

We have lived in a delicate balance between heritage and hatred. We have arrived at this moment having passed through years of segregation and racial prejudice. Descendants of slaves and slave owners look at flags and monuments through different eyes and feel different emotions of another time. Descendents of Union and Confederate soldiers now pledge a nonsectarian allegiance to one flag and one nation. Southern Conservatives have finally found a rational compromise in their party affiliation and found a voice without the comedic images of stentorian Southern demagogues. Southern Liberals are beginning to mature beyond our epic decade of sit-ins and freedom rides.

Now we look at our history without regional or racial bias. Once separated in our schools and at our dinner tables or by battle flags of a divided nation, we have become one people. Some of us who are Southern and white by birth may feel some uneasiness when we see Confederate symbols on flagpoles, courthouses, lapels, and pickup trucks. We still struggle to preserve and promote our heritage without the shackles of resistance to time and logic. We healed a nation divided by regional and racial bloodletting. We can easily find a common voice in a town, county, or region now divided only in our interpretation of our historical transition.

12

The Nouns and Adjectives of Extremism

Who would have ever thought that the adjectives *conservative* and *liberal* would become epithets to demonize those with whom we differ? As a matter of clarity, I prefer the terms *left* and *right* over the more ambiguous *conservative* and *liberal*. When we added prefixes and suffixes to imply extremism (*e.g.*, far-left, far-right, right wing, left wing) we took away their innocence. However, those references of disrespect have given respectability to the personified and capitalized nouns *Left* and *Right* when used without the modifiers of ridicule and condemnation.

None of us should ever have to feel it necessary to apologize for an idea, for fear of censure from Liberal or Conservative intimidation. I would suggest that we accept the reality of Left and Right being the two valid political and cultural philosophies that compete for the minds and hearts of our citizenry and promote the principles of democracy.

We need some methodology to eliminate the image of extremism and to provide equal dignity to each. For example, if you like alliteration, I would suggest the combinations Rational Right and Logical Left. These adjectives are praiseworthy and have almost identical meanings, and they are easy to remember for the media, spoken or written. These adjectives have obvious limitations and safeguards, in that they would not include any person or idea that is not rational or logical.

Nonrational and illogical persons and ideas would still be accessible to the public without censorship. Talk radio and cable news, if for no reason other than ratings, would still be staffed with those personalities and guests. Current opinion leaders of pulpits, classrooms, and the public podium would not be denied their audiences. No writer would be denied the freedom to publish a book just because it did not meet minimum standards of literacy or verity.

We might have to discontinue using *Christian* and *Religious* as adjectives of inclusion and exclusion, and recognize the Left and Right within any religious group. Faith, hope, charity, caring for widows and orphans, and keeping oneself unspotted from the world, fit neatly into either Left or Right. Spiritual and secular are mutually exclusive but not adversarial along lines of Left and Right. Acts of violence and torture in the name of a deity have no place in either camp.

Politically, we might change our two major parties to Left and Right. Southern Democrats and New England Republicans could then find some harmony of conscience and voter demographics.

Those not included would become part of splinter groups, a third and fourth party that would continue to advocate the ideas that have eroded the dignity of current partisan politics. In times of fear and unrest, either of these could become a plurality, creating a chaotic electoral balance in which the President would be chosen by the House or the Supreme Court.

I don't understand all of the conflicting positions on war, taxes, deficits, immigration, earmarks, church and state, gun rights, reproductive rights, and the many other issues that divide us. The rational debate on our body of laws and interpretation of moral values has been subverted by a vocabulary of extremist expletives.

The Rational Right and the Logical Left may eventually prevail as viable alternatives to our current polarized political and religious options. This could facilitate a great awakening of philosophical tolerance and moral behavior. Reason and logic could find voices in our international forum if heads of state rejected the language of malevolence. Clerics of all religions might avoid words that promote anger and retaliatory acts of violence inconsistent with the teachings of their respective faiths.

It is easier to feel good about being in a political party, a church, a country, or wearing a name or label, if you are hearing a consensus of approval and words of respect. Our verbal abuse with ill-chosen nouns could become less hurtful if we temper our language with a better choice of adjectives.

13

Finding Peace in the War on Christmas

My earliest images of Christmas were formed within a family of retailers. I spent much of my youth in the toy departments of two five-and-ten-cent stores, Rose's and later Jenkins' Ben Franklin. I learned about the market relationship of toy displays and the consumer preferences of children. Christmas morning was for me an affirmation of my youthful faith in yuletide folklore, and a well-planned inventory of dolls, toy guns, and baseball gloves.

Christmas was not part of my religious background in the Church of Christ. Being neither Protestant, Catholic, nor Jew, I was not aware of the forty or more days designated for religious observance. We were immersed in the death, burial, and resurrection of Jesus, but our doctrinal literalism gave me no certainty about the exact season of our Savior's birth. We questioned the spiritual importance of December 25 and observed a more secular recognition of a national holiday and an economic windfall for retailers.

Christmas was about family and the joy and love of giving and receiving gifts. It was an affirmation of peace on Earth and good will toward men. The birth of Jesus was part of my biblical truth, but not linked to a seasonal celebration.

The retail season has expanded, stretching from the candy corn of Halloween to early January markdowns of over-hyped designer labels. Stores have begun to rethink marketing strategy and approach a changing customer base with a more inclusive phrase—*Happy Holidays*. Many members of the religious and political right condemned this change as an ominous victory for secularists and politically correct elitists. Retailers and discounters, corporate and private, weighed a difficult public relations choice. Should they appeal to a religiously diverse market, and in doing so, risk the economic impact of a potential boycott by evangelical activists?

Talk radio and Fox News convinced listeners and viewers that there was a deliberate and organized war on Christmas. Every time we heard or looked at a seasonal commercial, we checked to see if it contained the traditional Merry Christmas or a more secular and ambiguous message. We checked the public square and the judicial buildings for sightings of Joseph and Mary and Baby Jesus. The presence or absence of religious displays was interpreted as some attack on the First Amendment or somebody's freedom of religion.

America is a secular nation, permitting no religious test for holding public office nor making laws establishing religion. Christmas is a holiday of choice for a majority of Americans. As such, it should never be subjected to restriction nor empowerment by government. Whether it should be a secular national holiday could be debated. Many in the conservative religious community misread the removal of religious icons from public places as an attack on individual freedom. Most liberal Christians saw this as a victory for tolerance and separation of the secular from the spiritual.

Inside the home and in front yards, Christians and other people of faith are free to worship and display the sacred symbols of their faiths. This freedom to worship is not challenged within the walls of the church, synagogue, or mosque. It is only when we move sectarian symbols to the public square that the voices of confrontation distract us from the peace and love of the season.

The Christmas (or holiday) season is the heartbeat of capitalism and the soul of structured spirituality. During this season of worship and shopping, I enjoy my freedom to greet and exchange smiles with my fellow Christians or my Jewish friends with a sincere Merry Christmas or Happy Hanukkah without fear of offending.

Sometimes we cannot know the content of someone's mind or the passion of the heart or understand other cultures and faiths, making our choice of appropriate greetings uncertain. I would hope that we feel no less warmth or sincerity and no less kinship in the human family when we smile and wish for someone a more secular or generic—Happy Holidays.

14

THINKING AND PRAYING OUT LOUD

Once a month I participate in something that has been designated as a Moment of Silence. When this was initially introduced in schools, its advocates defined it as a time to reflect, pray, meditate, or engage in any other silent activity. I have never known if I should bow my head or stand erect or have my eyes open or closed. Should my facial expression reflect the pain and suffering of humanity, or should it be an expression of my delight in being part of the education of the children of Williamson County?

At our school board meetings, the Moment of Silence follows the Pledge of Allegiance, which since 1954 has included a religious reference to a nation under God. Both of these observances have unfortunately become part of our constitutional debate on what is required and what is permitted in the bilateral impositions of religion and government.

From an intellectual and philosophical view it is difficult to distinguish between thinking and praying. I grew up believing that we were to pray without ceasing, which would suggest more of an attitude than a matter of audible verbiage. Individual prayer does not require the language skills and eloquence needed to stand at a podium or pulpit and lead a public prayer. Leading a public prayer in church or at a civic club meeting is a unique form of public speaking, in that you have a captive audience, but at the same time, and more importantly, you are talking to God.

When I am making speeches or writing editorials, I hope that my audience or readers would agree with most of my thoughts, but I usually include a few sentences that they might think are either confusing or confrontational. This is not appropriate in public prayer. Several years ago I began declining most invitations to lead a prayer in front of any audience that is predominantly Republican, conservative, or fundamentalist. I can speak from my heart for the lives and safety of our military, but I can't express my passionate opposition to the Iraqi war. I can speak from my heart asking God to bless the President or the Congress, but I cannot appeal to God for their defeat and removal from office. I can speak from my heart for the poor in spirit and the peacemakers, but I cannot question insensitive and harmful decisions made by our government.

There is a story I heard in which a prominent public figure was asked to give a prayer at a Presidential dinner. He stood at the podium for a minute or two in total silence. When he returned to his seat at the head table, President Lyndon Johnson leaned toward him and expressed concern that he had not been able to hear what he had said. To which he replied, "Mr. President, I wasn't talking to you."

The Moment of Silence came as a reaction to recent court decisions regarding government-sanctioned mandatory prayer in public schools. We see bumper stickers and listen to talk radio and the Religious Right all insisting that we should return prayer to our schools. That idea is frightening. Twelve or fewer elected people of whatever religion or ideology would write that prayer. Who am I to compose words that could express the religious thoughts of your children? I should never have the authority to mandate the recitation of any sectarian utterance in school. Government-mandated prayer, thought, or silence is seldom beneficial or advisable.

The purpose of prayer is to communicate with God or other controlling power. Some people prefer thinking rather than praying. I believe God listens to thinking. When we convince our children, our elected officials, or whoever might be listening, to think good thoughts, good things usually happen, and God's world becomes a better place. It's still okay to pray out loud whether you are talking to God or the folks on the back row.

15

ENGLISH: OUR LANGUAGE OF CHOICE AND NECESSITY

I am forever grateful to teachers of English who convinced me that nouns, verbs, and commas are not just rules but the interlocking pieces of intellectual civility. My grandmother taught me that words, with or without eloquence, are meaningless without sincerity and truth, and that they are our only weapons in the war against the confusion of Babel.

In 1993, a group of local literary patrons established the Council for the Written Word to promote writing and the accomplishments of Williamson County authors. In the first year, through a lot of research, they located and compiled information on 98 persons who had lived in the county, past and present, and had written and published a complete work of literature. Through continuing research, we now have documentation of approximately 400 local authors. Getting to know and working with published writers has intensified my appreciation of the English language.

Recently, I had lunch with a young lady in the food court at Cool Springs Galleria. She is an eight-year-old second-grader, born in China, who came to America three years ago. We had an interesting conversation covering whatever subjects she chose, just casual talk. During the twenty or twenty-five minute visit, I did not hear a single mistake in her grammar, her pronunciation, or her sentence structure in her non-native language that she has been taught in our public school system.

In that I do not speak Chinese, her skill in a second language enabled our conversational relationship. Those who are blessed with native or acquired multi-lingual skills have great advantage in a global society. Their career opportunities and ability to understand other cultures are greatly enhanced. Because of trends in immigration, we may have given too much of our attention to Spanish for pragmatic reasons. Whether immigration is a burden or essential to our economy is still an emotional debate. Interaction in labor, retail, school, church, and other areas, provide both necessity and opportunity for teaching and learning a second language. However, any nation without a commonality of language is a nation divided.

Some have suggested that the ability to speak and read English should be a legal requirement for citizenship. This might also necessitate some measurable standard of literacy, which could at some level become an infringement of human rights. The inability to read and write English is a sufficient impediment without the imposition of official sanction or rejection.

There is within this diversity of language an inherent temptation for elitism and ridicule. Comedy routines and political jokes are replete with examples of lingual ineptitude and our regional and ethnic identifiers. Whether we are writing a scholarly volume or sharing a casual conversation in a shopping mall, we are judged rightly or wrongly by our language skills.

As I listened to the questions and answers of my young Chinese-born friend, I became aware that I was listening to English in its purest form, taught by the dedicated and skilled teachers at Liberty Elementary. She may never be listed among our published writers nor become a noted orator, but the barrier of language has been removed from her life in America.

Bill Peach

Most English dictionaries give two definitions for the word *literate*. One is a matter of survival; the other, most of us never achieve. Speakers of English, our official or chosen language, are representative of every skill level between the two definitions. To make literacy a requirement of citizenship or qualifier for voting is too ambiguous to legislate. We can make those judgments when recording grades or awarding diplomas because we have established mandatory incremental levels of achievement for second grade or a graduate thesis. In the finality of assigning value, we learn that words are the essential components from which we make poetry, music, the oratory of diplomacy and academia, and the sincerity and truth of lasting friendships.

16

Ripples of Blue in a Puddle of Red

I don't think "being different" was something I chose for any pragmatic reason. I neither saw it as a badge of honor nor as an impediment to important goals. In a small-town retail environment, divergent speech was discouraged. In a fundamentalist church, some questions were never asked.

Opposition to ill-chosen wars was inconsistent with the patriotism of the previous generation. I was out of the loop with many of my white friends in discussions and jokes about race and segregation. Most public offices were not open to the mislabeled few. Apathy toward Civil War history and battle reenactments often cost me a seat at the table of historical academia. It was later in my adulthood that embracing the designation Democrat or Liberal became the ultimate stigma of incomprehension.

Everything I have ever written has contained some inkling of ambiguity to avoid open confrontation. On several occasions I have considered writing some definitive treatise on being different and the consequences of incongruent thought. One of my closest Republican friends, Hugh DuPree, encouraged me to write such a piece from the viewpoint of a Democrat. I tried, but I found that the thoughts that shaped my identity transcended party affiliation. Party affiliation seemed superficial.

I believe ethics and logic, not partisanship, should be the final determinants of label or perception.

Elections come every even-numbered year, reminding us that, in Williamson County, Democrats are drops of blue in a puddle of red. The only variables are turnout and vote-total percentages. I have watched our state legislators introduce and pass legislation that defies reason. I have watched school boards, county commissions, and elected city officials make decisions that are outside the range of my short list of priorities. I have watched preachers encourage congregations to support candidates on issues that have no beneficial or compatible relationship to Christian principles. I have watched candidates combine mediocrity and conservatism into an art form of invincibility.

The elections of 2006 and 2008 did not presage a Democratic revolution. The Republican Party moved farther to the right, and Democrats found new candidates and new voters in a more moderate and rational mood. Democrats took control of the House, Senate, and White House. Republicans retook our state legislature. In Williamson County, Democrats increased their numbers and their vocal and visual presence to hang on to their 30% minority status.

I don't know who painted our political demography in vibrant and clear colors of red and blue, with our coasts being blue and fly-over America being a vastness of red. We attach those colors not only to party affiliation, but to wedge issues that divide us philosophically and theologically. By whatever configuration of interpretation, I have come to know that my favorite color is blue.

The mural of life in America is ever so slightly more blue than red. We have cast off the gaudy shades of chromatic extremist obscenity, and found a national personality that has pockets of center/left and center/right in hues of inoffensive shadings that portray a landscape of tranquility. Tennessee is a palette of reds and blues, more reds than blues, divided by a river and a plateau, and rural and urban disparities. Williamson County is decidedly red, but tempered by tolerance and commonality of purpose.

I miss the days when my friend Hugh DuPree was chairman of the Williamson County Republican Partly. We could sit together and have a rational conversation about what it is like to be different in Williamson County. It is still hard to explain my thoughts on a lot of unasked and unanswered questions, but being a Democrat has lost any residual stigma of second-class citizenship. The jokes about counting Williamson County Democrats on the fingers of one hand have all gone away. What were once a few drops of blue in a puddle of red have become waves of concentric ripples within a larger ocean of blue.

17

Bang the Drum Softly

When we see televised anti-war or peace rallies, the cameras usually show repeated images of Jane Fonda and Susan Sarandon and the traditional entourage of preachers, veterans, and aging flower-children. The protesters carry print-shop placards with axioms of anger and crayon-quality expressions of personal pain. Following our last casualty in Vietnam, anti-war rallies sort of went out of favor. I don't know if we lost our taste for them, or just forgot why.

I have never been to a big protest rally of any kind. I didn't attend any when I was younger, not even the concert at Woodstock. I wouldn't have been offended by the love, sex, or music, but I have never liked mud, drugs, or substandard toilet facilities. People at rock concerts and anti-war rallies in the Sixties usually wore tacky clothes—either ragged, dirty, or tie-dyed.

I don't remember ever having attended anything called a pro-war rally. I was only nine when World War II ended with our victories over Japan and Europe. In our neighborhood, we were celebrating the end of the war, not so much the war itself. More recently, wars have had no winners. Both sides have found some acceptable benchmark balance of compassion, carnage, and futility, and have quit before either side could declare victory or defeat.

Politics, Preaching & Philosophy

I can't explain the difference between rallies, protests, demonstrations, and celebrations. There is the diametric of being for or against something. There is an inherent contingent relationship between any idea and its implied antithesis. One man's allegiance is another's treason; one man's crusade is another's inquisition. Heroes and fanatics are not always identified by universal standards of bravery and lunacy.

We should not interpret our not attending a protest as opposition to the event that attracted the crowd. If multitudes of peaceniks march on the Mall, or thousands of flag-waving patriots line the sidewalks on the Fourth of July, or Southern Baptists fill the Sommet Center, our presence or absence is neither a requisite nor disqualifier for respectability. I don't feel any guilt about missing a march on Washington, a Civil War remembrance, or a religious revival.

As I have grown older, I have lost some enthusiasm for standing and cheering with thousands of emotionally charged people. During my college days I braved rain and bone-chilling temperatures in a crowded football stadium. The excitement was geographic, quasi-academic, and to some degree, just festive tailgate revelry. Like football, political storming of ramparts is not conducive to neutrality and often not consistent with rational decorum. Today I watch NCAA and NFL championship games in channel-surfing fragments.

I am proud of being an American, a Christian, an alumnus of Middle Tennessee State University, and a fan of the Titans. I delight in the comfort of gatherings of unanimity at all levels. We are a nation that loves the commonality of philosophical, political, and mundane similitude. Even in our democracy, dissent is discouraged and endangered.

I feel out of place at any monolithic gathering of concerned Republicans, Conservatives, or sectarian Fundamentalists. The same is true in the company of Jane Fonda, Susan Sarandon, preachers, hippies, and radicals who gather in public places to protest wars and other human obscenities. I avoid any mob that might storm the public square to wave or burn a flag or a cross.

Obviously, since I don't hate my country, or the President, the military, white people, Muslims, evangelicals, or the Supreme Court, I find little cause for organized protest or demonstrative outrage. I spend a lot of time at small anti-war or peace rallies, often by myself, with no placards, no shouting, no crowds. Anytime you find me hanging out in Downtown Franklin or the mall, you have the potential for a peace rally, just you and me. Join me and share your thoughts and your words. We may have missed our last chance for peace among nations and cultures, but wherever two or more are gathered, peace is attainable on a smaller scale.

18

EDUCATION: OUR RIGHT OR RESPONSIBILITY

The common schools in New England were established in colonial days by Calvinists who passed laws requiring parents to educate and catechize their children in accordance with biblical principles. These schools were supported by the townspeople and run by the clergy. To the Calvinists, education without God was unthinkable. After a long history of conflict between Catholic and Protestant, between orthodoxy and a compromised nondenominational curriculum, public education evolved into a secular education run by the government.

An agrarian lifestyle, without the benefit of advanced farm and household technology, created a need for a family-farm labor force and childcare by older siblings. We found ways to fit the learning season into and around the growing season. Planting and harvesting defined the school year. The oldest or brightest of the male children were marked and destined for leadership. Their siblings were destined for farming or factory work, or bearing and raising children. Education was not for all.

Immigration of Europeans became controversial, in that ethnic groups, many being Catholic, were not learning English and were concentrating in ghetto enclaves in larger cities. Conflict between parents and government over the education of children most often involved child labor, immigration, biblical instruction, and sectarian diversity.

In 1852, Massachusetts enacted the first state compulsory school-attendance law. By 1929, all states had passed similar statutes, including Tennessee in 1905. The purpose of these laws was to ensure that every child be educated. Interestingly, compulsory attendance does not equate with academic achievement. Legislators and educators have established and revised curriculum requirements, standardized testing, teacher certification and professional development, and textbook content in an effort to teach and quantify the mastery and retention of certain facts and skills that we all deem essential for a desired quality of life.

In my school years at Boston and Hillsboro, we accepted the logic or constitutional right of government to require that all children in a designated age range attend school a designated number days each year. My grandmother taught me the ethical truths of rural morality, but dutifully waved me off to a bus that would take me to a world of math, science, history, and literature, which I would share with her at the end of the school day.

Recently, the idea of leaving no child behind was codified into something that we now refer to as No Child Left Behind, which mandates ambitious, maybe impossible, test scores for students in every identifiable subgroup. Public schools are required to test all students, regardless of language skills, special needs, or family income. The law also dictates that public school teachers not only be certified, but highly qualified, with certification by grade level and subject. My concern is that there are lesser standards of accountability for families who choose to opt out of public schools.

Just weeks ago, a local newspaper did a feature article on a method of home-schooling which the parent referred to as un-schooling. The methods seemed innovative, but un-schooling has a long tradition. One paragraph heading read that one of the children liked books but did not read. The child was nine years old and did not read.

The debate over compulsory education did not end in 1929. Politicians and parents either defend or condemn public education to validate their personal choices of public or alternative education. Williamson County is blessed with two exemplary public school districts, excellent private schools, and a dedicated group of home-school parents. The irony is that, when a social unit assumes the right to educate a child, it also assumes the responsibility to educate that child, and if it fails its responsibility, it may also forfeit that right.

I am a strong advocate for a parent's right to choose an alternative to public education. I am saddened when any child is left behind, either by a multicultural and secular government school, or by a loving and protective parent with good intentions and limited teaching skills.

19

ON INNOCENCE AND HUMILITY

In our earliest images of Christianity, we see a symbolic presence of children. Holy writings and subsequent religious art depict Jesus surrounded or followed by children. In His teachings we are admonished to be as little children as an implied attribute of human behavior or a requisite of divine approval. In the Beatitudes, those persons specifically designated as blessed are the peacemakers, the meek, the merciful, and the pure in heart. Early Christians lived in subjugation to Roman persecution and its unholy alliance with Judaic orthodoxy. Humility and innocence were Christianity's earliest weapons of survival.

Rome was converted to Christianity, and with the benefit of government sanction, Christianity lost its innocence and its humility and became the captive of that which it had conquered. Centuries later, a simple treatise nailed to the door of a church was a unique act of courage of an oppressed people who overthrew a corrupt religious and political power and became a diverse and disheveled body of believers. The Reformation succeeded in its quest for freedom of religion, which led to the establishment of many churches, which may or may not have been the intent or image of early Christianity. However, this balance of unanimity, diversity, and tolerance has enabled its survival.

Politics, Preaching & Philosophy

Through two world wars, American and European Christians have, for brief periods, taken up the sword in active combat. Pacifist Christians have received the benefits of residence within nations friendly to religious freedom. After each war, the conquering nations reached into their biblical roots and treated the vanquished with dignity and benevolence and forgave the timidity of the noncombatant.

Historically, Christianity has shaped the civil governance and cultural behavior of America and other countries within which it had a presence. Conversely, the government and culture of each nation or region has shaped the image of Christianity within its borders or jurisdiction. Most people believe that the excessive influence of either poses a threat to the other. In that Christianity is encumbered by its inherent innocence and humility, the advantage in any open confrontation would be on the side of government and the culture that sustains that government.

There have been shifts in the balance of power. Some were the result of cultural changes; some were effected by legislative or judicial action. Many of these changes resulted from rational dialogue among people of faith who were committed to a secular government within which religious freedom could exist without sanction or interference.

Throughout history, the voices of innocence and humility have often gone unheard during periods dominated by enemies of religion or religious zealots reacting to that opposition. From this conflict, the most audible voices of Christianity are often those of charlatans who display neither innocence nor humility. Some reach prominence through television, some through evangelical charisma, some through the seduction of the spiritually weak. Others find influence within the political structure by taking politics to the pulpit, and taking religion to the halls of government.

We may yet encounter military battles and sectarian acts of violence between Christianity and other more radical and cruel religions, putting us at risk of massive destruction and carnage. We may be shouted down and ridiculed by a segment of the populace openly hostile to any religion. We could also lose our humility and innocence in the cultural ambiguity that may make Christianity indistinguishable from national arrogance.

A great number of people cling to, or yearn for, the innocence and humility of early Christianity. Many still believe the meek may yet inherit the Earth. Eventually, Christianity, or some ideology that embodies similar moral principles, will survive. Most Christians believe this to be God's plan. This may be accomplished by world dominance by either an empire or alliance of nations within which a compassionate or benevolent religion can survive. Innocence and humility may rise to power from the wreckage and ashes of human folly.

Arrogant Christianity is easily defeated; humble Christianity is invincible.

20

Retail: A Profession, or Product, or Price

On the Saturday and Sunday of our annual Main Street Festival, I walked the retail district of Historic Downtown Franklin. Earlier on Saturday, I had worked five hours in my professional role as an itinerate adjunct men's clothier for a national chain retailer in the Cool Springs Galleria mall.

Last week, I received a thank-you note from a Dillard's customer. It read in part, "Thank you for the time you spent with me helping me upgrade my wardrobe. The level of service you provided was exemplary and is rare in today's marketplace. Thanks again for the sage advice."

With those words still resonating to remind me of my retail days on Main Street, I walked into tasteful and innovative shops and talked to owners and managers who continue the tradition that shaped my life and retail philosophy. The singular thing that I miss most in Downtown Franklin is seeing the names of proprietors on storefronts. In earlier days, in an eclectic array of signage, we identified our businesses with a combination label that offered not only a category of essential merchandise, but the name of a retailer who served the community as a professional.

Today we have in Downtown Franklin a new wave of those professionals. They spend their waking hours and invest their capital in the difficult role of individual entrepreneurship, which we have almost lost in a changing retail environment. In moments when I feel some concern about their youth and inexperience, I remember that I arrived on Main Street at the age of fifteen, and invested my first dollars and chaired a merchant organization at twenty-six.

With reluctance, we accept the truth that Historic Downtown Franklin is a limited supplier of basic consumer products. The simple logistics of square footage has driven that service to the ubiquitous boxes of chain identity. In order to compete in this reality, merchants have to find that comparative advantage essential to all successful businesses.

Retailing is composed of an inexplicable combination of service, selection, and price. Textbooks define retailers as providers of time, place, quantity, and utility of products. The history and traditions of Franklin have blessed our merchants and continue to treat them as professionals. Whether or not you personally find a need for chocolate, antiques, furniture, live music, complicated coffee, pizza, kinky clothing, or useless trinkets of vanity, Historic Downtown Franklin is a place like no other. We have retained our skills in and devotion to the marketing of uniqueness.

In the big-box world of national retailers, they (or we, as I have had to learn to think) must make difficult comparative corporate decisions about service, selection, and price. Chains struggle with the conflict of perception and reality. Department stores can and do provide a professional level of customer service equal to that of Main Street, but they do so at the risk of losing customers to the bottom-feeding tactics of deceptive pricing and ambiguous standards of quality. Consequently, upscale retailers play games with suggested retail prices and markdowns, and in so doing have alienated a generation of merchants offended by designer labels, promotional gimmicks, and nontraditional images of price and quality.

In the first full year Cool Springs Galleria was open, our county sales-tax revenue doubled. To try to wish away price-driven, designer-label, made-in-China retailing is anachronistically futile and economically not realistic.

As I move between and within the contrasting cultures of Cool Springs and Downtown Franklin, I find it much like having dual citizenship in worlds that are geographically five miles apart and philosophically disconnected beyond even Darwinian explanation.

When you shop in the mall, you do find professional retailers. Some are very old with a lifetime of retail; some are very young and ambitious and innocently at risk of disenchantment. In Historic Downtown Franklin, retailing is still a highly respected profession, driven by ownership, not just by product and price.

21

The Blind Men and the Elephant

Six blind men from Indostan touched the several parts of an elephant—the side, the tusk, the trunk, the knee, the ear, and the tail. Each avowed with certainty that an elephant was very like—a wall, a spear, a snake, a tree, a fan, and a rope. Long before I had read this poem by John Godfrey Saxe, I had heard it in narration as a parable with meaning beyond the simple anatomy of an elephant. I was not aware of the final stanza of the poem, which reads—

> So oft in theologic wars,
> The disputants, I ween,
> Rail on in utter ignorance
> Of what each other mean,
> *And prate about an Elephant*
> *Not one of them has seen!*

I don't know what passions or uncertainties of the writer invoked this metaphorical reference to theology and blindness in the same literary document.

My impressions of religion are limited to the Christian faith and were shaped in my early years in a one-room building in southern Williamson County. Having grown up in a fundamentalist church, like others of a similar upbringing I feel a continuing imperative to defend my faith of choice and concurrently explain and apologize for the historical human frailties of Southern rural fundamentalism.

On Sunday mornings, our body of truth was sufficient for instruction and edification. The good men who occupied the pulpit were often schooled in secular knowledge, but reluctant to explore ideas unfamiliar to their audience. The boundaries of our public school education were often fixed by the accepted truth of the previous generation. The ensuing travesty of this is the myth that biblical fervor and intellect are inversely proportional. To illustrate this, I share a thought from the late Doug Marlette, cartoonist and creator of *Kudzu*. He avows that he was raised in a small town that was so remote and rustic, that even the Presbyterians handled snakes and spoke in tongues.

At our church, we often defined who we were by proclaiming who we were not. We distanced ourselves from those whom we collectively called Holy Rollers. We believed that we had culturally and academically risen above signs and wonders and unknown tongues. We also looked with equal distrust upon men and women of learning who rejected the recorded Acts of early Christians and arrived at their truth through the wisdom of man taught at secular universities. Our greatest fear was that worldly knowledge would cause our children to forsake the faith.

As I have grown older I have become more convinced that faith and reason are not only compatible, but that each is stronger when reinforced by the strength of the other. This is an idea I have had the privilege of sharing in pulpits and classrooms of both conservative and liberal churches. Conservative churches tend to build on faith and validate with reason, while liberal churches build on reason and fill the inexplicable with faith.

As I touch the many parts of religion, I come to believe that it is not easily defined by its separate parts. As I watch the televangelists in the massive arenas who prey upon tens of thousands, I am reminded of the New Testament metaphor of wolves in sheep's clothing. I watch religious intrusion into politics, and I see the monsters and dragons of John's Revelation. Other times I see a seductive serpent, a wily fox, a hovering vulture, a trampling horse, or a lowly beast of burden awaiting its destined mission into Jerusalem. In mainstream churches, religion is much like the mother hen who gathers her chicks under her wings. Most of the time, I see contemporary Christendom in a tranquil pasture, lying without fear beside a lion, or sometimes beside a lamb.

The six blind men from Indostan should not be condemned for their reliance on tactile sense and elemental interpretation. Their conclusions were consistent with their own human experience. No one could or should question the accuracy or the sincerity of their certainty. Elephants and religion are complex animals.

22

ON THE FAIRNESS DOCTRINE

Recently, some Republican and Democrat senators expressed concern over the perceived excessive influence of conservative talk radio. Some went so far as to suggest the return to the Fairness Doctrine. Those of us who find Rush Limbaugh, Bill O'Reilly, and Sean Hannity outside the parameters of rational thought should never, in honesty with our liberal philosophy, support any government intervention that would inhibit the free exchange of ideas in the broadcast marketplace.

From 1949 until 1987 we empowered the Federal Communications Commission to enforce, or attempt to enforce, an ill-conceived Fairness Doctrine. Under the theory that radio and television were licensed entities, the licensing agency had the right or obligation to demand balanced views on controversial issues. After much debate, ambiguous legislation, presidential vetoes, and a series of judicial decisions, we reached the consensus that fairness in the media is adequately served by the multiplicity of voices in the marketplace.

Members of the liberal community are frustrated that we have not been able to establish a presence on talk radio. Because of limited scheduling and low signal, I don't bother to search for liberal radio. Most of my commutes range from 2.2 to 4.1 miles, and drive-time radio is a low priority for me.

I have conceded radio to the Right and listen most frequently to local news or light rock.

With a remote and a satellite dish, I surf between C-SPAN (350) and Fox News (360), occasionally switching to NPT, CNN, and Headline News. I am encouraged by the war of words between Fox News and the other networks, erasing the image of domination by liberal television. We are intelligent enough to know that the "fair and balanced" claim is contingent upon the diversity of voices and is not a single network assemblage of monolithic punditry. Also, we accept the fact that television hosts control the clock and assume the right to define the moment in their closing remarks.

The debate continues as to whether or not a station or network can or should cancel a program or dismiss a personality which or whom the public and sponsors find objectionable. We understand that the offensive voices are hired for market appeal and fired when the offensiveness crosses the line of accepted standards of decency. How do we explain the exit of a Don Imus type without trying to justify the entry? The same applies to all voices of absurdity and defamation. But still, I usually find repression of speech more offensive than the content of speech.

I think the ineffectiveness of any attempt at government-sanctioned mandate or restraint on radio or television is a result of our inability to define freedom of speech. We have exhibited a greater fear of print censorship than other media restrictions. Also, print media has been less inclined to push the edge of decency and decorum. We have come to accept obscene printed words when disguised with three hyphens or asterisks, but decry audible and visual obscenity during family television primetime. From this self-discipline, newspapers have escaped philosophical or cultural censorship, whether or not we see them as purveyors of liberal or conservative bias.

The only intrusion of government into media that I might advocate is that of limiting ownership. If a few powerful corporations or individuals are allowed to acquire and own a disproportional share of newspapers, television, radio, or combinations thereof, we risk the loss of that multiplicity of voices essential to our democracy.

A member of my family gave me a gift certificate to a local bookstore. After a long search, I chose *Blasphemy: How the Religious Right Is Hijacking Our Declaration of Independence* by Alan Dershowitz. I looked at titles of books written by proponents of the Religious Right. Maybe in fairness I should have bought one of those also. But then I thought—they need to be on a shelf in a bookstore. Sitting on the bookstore shelf, they do no harm to anyone.

23

THE PHILOSOPHY OF ANTITHESES

In our contrarian culture, the prestige of the antithesis may have exceeded that of the thesis. For every idea or belief held by the few or the many, there is an opposite or competing antithesis to which media usually give preferential coverage. A thesis, which requires some inkling of validity, relies on the advantage of affirmation, which is often offset by the volatility of the counter-argument, which requires little or no proof for its equal status.

We have framed our antithetical language by attaching the prefix *anti-* to anything that anyone has found to be objectionable or dangerous. In some instances we even eliminate the hyphen, to create single-word expressions of unquestioned antipathy, such as *antipathy* and *antitheses*.

Our rules of grammar and punctuation dictate when or if we hyphenate compound words. We have built our language on Greek and Latin roots by adding prefixes and suffixes, extending our words well beyond the two-syllable norm of Southern conversation. Hyphens help to eliminate the absurdity and clumsiness of antidisestablishmentarianism for definition and justification of right margins.

When I looked in the dictionary, I found antiadministration, but when I tried to write it, my word processor only accepted a hyphenated anti-administration. I found the same resistance to proadministration, allowing only the hyphenated pro-administration. It does seem logical that prefixes designating approval and opposition be treated equally when written.

We have found that we can discredit dissent by adding *anti* (with a hyphen) to those words that we have all come to embrace as our own (*e.g.*, American, Christian, democracy, environment, faith, family, choice, life, education, military, freedom, privacy). Equally effective is the other perspective of adding *pro* (also with a hyphen) to those ideas that we all obviously know to be unfit for human endorsement (war, hatred, tyranny, ignorance, abortion, death, taxation, monopoly, etc.).

Problems arise when we reverse these designations to inaccurately or ambiguously define our own affirmations. Anti-war has validity during specific conflicts, but may not equate pacifism. Pro-life is usually not considered relevant to capital punishment, and is more often translated as pro-birth. Being pro-choice could relate to reproductive rights or parental preference for private-school vouchers or home-schooling.

Sometimes the ambiguity is used as a distraction to discredit. Nobody is pro-abortion or anti-choice. Advocates of euthanasia are not pro-death. We do not choose to be anti-environment, anti-defense, anti-justice, anti-peace, anti-education. If we are to conduct a civil discussion, we need to minimize the use of defamatory prefixes and more clearly define the root words.

One of the greater ironies of dialectic interaction is that many words have antithetical images based on ambiguous connotations of those same words. We use such words to convey virtue and defamation just as effectively as we do using prefixes. In essence, a word can be an antithesis in and of itself. Pacifism is a virtue or cowardice. Secular is a valid designation of nonsectarian neutrality or may be seen as an equation of anti-religious. The rich may be the financially successful or the greedy; the poor may be the lazy and inept, or God's directives for our compassion.

Some words are impervious to antithetical designation, but contingent on their implementation. America is some conciliatory combination of a republic and a democracy, based on the quantum division of our components. Democracy, in its simplest definition, is a government of majority, and has virtue only in pragmatic compassion, magnanimity, and sense of commonality. Otherwise it becomes a tyranny of the many.

With my apology to George Orwell, I would refer you to two cartoons that are imbedded in my memory. One is a scene in which a cow is presiding over an audience consisting of maybe a dozen or more cows and one horse. The chair-bovine says, "All in favor of the resolution, say *Moo*." The other is a scene in a pasture of a group of several wolves and one sheep preparing to take a vote on what to have for dinner.

24

JUDGING ONE'S COVER BY A BOOK

A recent poll by the Associated Press found that one in four adults had read no books in the past year. The poll found that people who *do* read averaged seven books a year. The books most often read were religious works and popular fiction. The poll did not indicate whether the same people read both.

One would assume that a book of popular fiction should be read completely, front to back, and it would have a climax or some resolution at or near the end. Religion and philosophy offer less sequential options. I have stacks of partially read books with bookmarks marking my progress as of last sitting. Since I have not finished them, I do not know how they will end. These books have no plot, no suspense, no conclusion. To be honest, I am not certain that I read a complete book last year.

After the publication of my book *Random Thoughts Left & Right*, my wife told someone that I had finished my third book. Jokingly, the person expressed concern that I was a slow reader. Ironically, I *am* a slow reader. My reading habits are neither voracious, avid, ravenous, nor insatiable. My passion is for learning, for which reading is a necessity. Reading takes us beyond our own introspective mischief and the triviality of casual conversation. Reading gives us exposure to persons who are more intelligent than our peers or ourselves.

Some of my partially read books have bookmarks in the first or second chapters. I am impressed when I watch a reader nearing the end of a novel of four-hundred-plus pages. Occasionally, I carry John Egerton's *Speak Now Against the Day*, which he admits is too long at 704 pages, but also regrets leaves out two important chapters. More than likely, I will never finish that book, but it continues to give me insight into an important period of Southern history.

As a fashion accessory, a book serves the same purpose as a laptop, iPod nano, briefcase, bracelet, or a dog. Last week, I initiated a conversation with a man carrying a biography of Albert Einstein. Validating my assumption that he was an academic, he turned out to be a university provost.

Can you judge a man or woman by a book cover? Do we choose our friends by the books they read? Do we make assumptions about intelligence, personality, moral values, religious and political preference by book titles? Yes, we do. Our associative conclusions may not always be accurate, depending on the reading diversity of that person.

Titles by Rick Warren, Joel Osteen, Jim Wallis, George Lakoff, or Christopher Hitchens can be indicators of one's belief system. Books by Ann Coulter, Bill O'Reilly, Hillary Clinton, Al Gore, or Barack Obama may suggest common interest or potential confrontation. Do we feel compelled to give advice and comfort to anyone reading a self-help book? Do we initiate a conversation with readers of romance novels, cookbooks, pet-grooming manuals, military history, computer tutorials, or economic forecasts?

One can't always know whether the reader would welcome conversation or prefer to be left alone to read in privacy. Books can serve both purposes. One can avoid unwelcome advances or boring conversation within the covers of a book. Others welcome the shared intellectual bond of having enjoyed the same book.

I felt such a bond as I watched a young man reading his Bible in a restaurant. With a yellow highlighter, he carefully marked specific verses. I assumed he was preparing for a Bible study group or Sunday school class. Later, when I walked past his table, I was surprised that he had highlighted the entirety of two opened pages. I wondered if that was his bookmark, measuring his perseverance and devotion to a book that he would eventually finish.

I sat down and opened *The Cambridge Dictionary of Philosophy*, with its subjects listed alphabetically, and finished reading the extended definition of *Aesthetics*. I may not finish this one this year.

25

ON BEING RELIGIOUSLY LITERATE

The passing of time has relegated Zeus and Jupiter to historical mythology and replaced them with the God of Greek Orthodoxy and Catholicism. I offer this not as an equation, but as a premise that religion is a major determinant of the philosophy and literature of any culture. As an English major, I came to appreciate the importance of Greek and Roman literature, but still do not understand the role of mythology and religion in early civilizations.

You and I live in a culture in which Christianity is the majority religion. In order to understand our culture, we should be conversant with the content of the Bible. The Old and New Testaments are the governing documents of two important religions. While they have no civil authority, they are often the interpretive adjudicators of sectarian thought in our daily conversations.

The number of people who choose not to identify with any religious tradition is growing. As fundamentalist emphasis on biblical inerrancy and literal interpretation intensifies, growth and retention rise and fall with logical proportion. Christianity is constantly changing in its emphasis of doctrine, worship, benevolence, politics, and standards of morality. Parents are challenged by questions from children exposed to diversity within their own religion. Non-Jewish parents need to know the history and significance of Jewish holy days based on our shared sacred document. Our community is no longer just Jewish and Christian, but increasingly influenced by Middle Eastern and Asian theology.

If you don't answer your children's religious questions, others will, and you may not like the answers they provide. Parents are children's first and primary religious educators. Where is Heaven? Where will I go when I die? Why don't Rachel and Benjamin believe in Christmas or Halloween? Am I saved? Why are some people going to Hell?

Within this framework, many parents are choosing alternatives to public education—private, parochial, or home schools. This decision is sometimes academic, sometimes religious, sometimes for protective parental nurturing.

In the field of public education, we have an obligation to teach *about* religion as a part of history and culture, but logic and law dictate that we should not *teach* any religion. As trustees of the scholastic population, school board members should not assume a role of advocacy in sectarian indoctrination. Holidays and events should be scheduled not as religious observances, but with pragmatic and conciliatory sensitivity to the religious and the non-religious.

Schools have the responsibility to teach and enforce moral and ethical behavior. This is part of citizenship under the aegis of secular law and the demeanor that sustains civilization. Whether or not this is derived from divine authority should be between parent and child. Some of the literature that we assign may include examples of inappropriate language and behavior, to teach the history of intolerance, prejudice, violence, promiscuity, profanity, and other offensive acts and attitudes. Each parent has the right to alternative reading selections, and also has the responsibility to reinforce universal values and discuss questions that arise from exposure to conflicting ideas.

Among the difficult questions for parents and educators are conflicts between ideas based on recent findings and those based on tradition and folklore. Some conflicts are residual from a Southern history of racial injustice, anti-intellectualism, and a propensity to violence, regional attitudes possibly perpetuated by Old Testament writings. On balance, most of our regional morality is sustained and enhanced by Bible-based faith. I was raised by a deeply religious grandmother who taught me that the New Testament was an adequate document for my spiritual well-being, but that secular intelligence was essential to any quest for ultimate truth.

Secular parents are also religious educators. Religious parents are also secular educators. Educators do not teach their religion of choice in the classroom, nor refute any part of any other belief system. Mathematics, science, history, geography, technology, government, and language arts are not religious subjects. Public education is secular. Answers to religious questions must come from houses of worship or from literate parents.

26

ONE NATION, DIVISIBLE

The issue of compelled speech has a long history in public school districts. Two cases that came before the Supreme Court, *West Virginia Board of Education v. Barnette* and *Minersville School District v. Gobitis,* involved Jehovah's Witness parents who objected to their children being required to recite the Pledge of Allegiance in school. Although children are allowed to opt out of the exercise, there have been incidents in which students were forced to stand outside in the rain or serve detention for refusing to recite the Pledge.

It is ironic that the Court struck down the West Virginia statute and upheld a similar flag-salute statute in Pennsylvania. After the *Minersville v. Gobitis* case, there was a wave of intolerance for Jehovah's Witnesses in many regions of the country. The Witnesses refused to salute the flag. These two cases went before the Court in 1940 and 1943 before the Pledge had become a religious document.

I would question the value of patriotic recitation in schools and the more recent inclusion of the phrase *under God*. We sometimes overlook the history of the Pledge and the issue of compelled speech. The simple question of whether or not a patriotic document should also include an affirmation of religion divides a nation of serious patriotic Christians who might interpret the Constitution or Bible differently.

The Pledge that I recited in school was the draft adopted in 1924 in which the words *my Flag* had been changed to *the Flag of the United States of America*. Francis Bellamy, the Baptist minister who wrote the original in 1892, opposed this change.

In 1954, fueled by the Cold War and the influence of McCarthyism, Congress felt it expedient to inject religion into the Pledge by inserting the words *under God*. There was debate at the time as to whether the wording of the First Amendment was violated by this change. Our Constitution forbids government from endorsing religious views, or practicing any establishment of religion. Some people simply objected to change, favoring the original without the pressure of transitory and whimsical political trends.

None of this would matter if no one were compelled to recite this Pledge. Tennessee law requires such a recitation in public schools with the option to not participate. The ambiguity comes from the question of how to not comply. Should a student leave the room, or remain seated, or stand and not say the words, or recite the Pledge in its original form prior to the 1954 change? In a typical local school environment, would the student be ridiculed or ostracized for nonconformity?

The Jehovah's Witnesses' refusal originated from their religious prohibition of pledging allegiance to a symbol of the government, considering this idolatry. In contrast, the current resistance comes primarily from religious people who find a conflict in pledging allegiance to a government that may not be compatible with their religious beliefs. This comes from many perceptions, including the involvement in an immoral war, or the erosion of religious freedom within a government perceived to be moving toward theocracy.

The other objection, and the one that receives the most publicity, is from non-theistic citizens who want to recite a patriotic expression without acknowledgement of a deity. It is unfortunate that public schools have been historically the crucible of debate in most questions of compelled speech. The Court decided in *Elk Grove Unified School District v. Newdow* not along the establishment clause issue, but ruled that Newdow did not have standing because of the mother's custodial and parental rights.

As we continue to debate this issue, and as we anticipate other Court cases, there are some factors we need to consider. Many people are not aware of the 1954 change. Some of our students prefer to recite the original Pledge without the recently added religious statement, while other students prefer to recite the amended version. It would be far better that we teach our children history, government, citizenship, religious tolerance, and the Constitution, and let patriotism come from the heart rather than the verbal monotony of religious or patriotic compulsion.

27

Divine Intervention

There is a story of an atheist who found himself facing a huge grizzly bear with no opportunity to escape. He fell to his knees and asked God to save him. After listening to God's reprimand for a life of disbelief, the atheist asked whether, if God would not save *him*, He might, then, convert the bear to Christianity. The facial expression of the bear became very tranquil, a passive serenity. The massive beast folded his paws and bowed his head and said, "Heavenly Father, we are thankful for this food we are about to receive."

Our spiritual sincerity is often interrupted by the comedic, but sometimes enlightening, attitudes toward divine intervention in human affairs. In local and national elections, candidates are often quoted as having made statements of implied attribution to God's will in the outcomes of our democratic process. A friend of mine who recently vacationed in Las Vegas asked that I wish her good luck and even requested my prayers. I prayed for her safety, but in my tradition in the Church of Christ, I could not imagine God's concern with the mechanical or human probabilities of the gaming devices of that seductive city. I even wondered if God might look down and question the fairness of His severity with some Old Testament urban centers of iniquity.

Politics, Preaching & Philosophy

As I cling to my spiritual affiliation with both the Church of Christ and the Unitarian Universalists, I meet and talk to people with quite different interpretations of God's role in their daily lives. I can understand a Methodist or Episcopalian, on a Sunday morning, thanking God for Vanderbilt's surprising victory over some rival. One could easily assign this anomaly to divine intervention, but footballs bounce funny.

Williamson County is a haven for life choices based on spiritual determinism. I listen to and read about poets, pickers, prophets, prospectors, and politicians who were called to seek fortune and opportunity in Franklin with God's endorsement and audible urging. I would never question the sincerity of those who hear the voice of a personal God, nor those who assign Old Testament prophetic certainty to the mundane and superficial unfolding of human events. My inability to comprehend does not imply disbelief. The silence in my head gives me no feeling of disfavor nor fear of failure.

Those of us who have a traditional history of fundamentalist Bible study and a secular formal education usually avoid polarities of contemporary religious practice. I fear being a part of an arrogance within which I would find delight in accomplishments and accolades with no humility and no appreciation for the metaphysical complexities over which I have no control. Nor would I want to be part of a lifestyle within which I would invoke the participation and endorsement of God in the foolish and selfish failures into which I have been led by my inability to interpret the ethical and logical truths of the standard rules of human civility.

We all share access to that body of knowledge we call truth. To some, truth comes from divine revelation—written, spoken, or imagined. To some, truth comes from logic, intellect, pragmatism, and spiritual contemplation—written, spoken, or imagined. The latter rarely comes with the assurance of certainty.

Much of the evil of human history has been perpetrated by evil men who attributed their personal and political ambitions to a calling beyond themselves. On a lesser scale, persons who view God as a constantly intercessional deity are at risk of invoking benign approval for trivial or less-than-noble human adventures.

Most of the good works of human compassion have been initiated and performed by disciples of the great religions of the world. My faith and biblical teaching lead me to believe that God is on the side of good and is an opponent of man's misguided folly. This would lead me to conclude that, in matters of good and evil, divine intervention can be beneficial.

28

The Reasonable Rhetoric of the Road

Sooner or later, it becomes necessary or logical to remove a bumper sticker. Then we are faced with scraping off the ugly residue from what was once a noble statement on behalf of humanity. For three years, I had questioned the need or wisdom to display the name of an unsuccessful 2004 candidate for President. After that, I chose to wear a lapel pin to support my 2008 candidate rather than a bumper sticker.

I had not removed my sticker of preference until late September of 2007. I kept it on as a subtle alternative to wording that might suggest denial of blame for any political result from the previous cycle. That is one consolation of losing. Imagine my displeasure and chagrin if my candidate had won and embarked on an ill-conceived mission for which I might now feel deep pain and guilt.

Some person, who may have disliked my candidate, inscribed a word that some might consider obscene on my bumper sticker for all the world to see. Decency demanded that the offending graffiti be removed. Luckily, the three-year-old relic peeled off, leaving no lasting evidence of political activism.

For weeks I drove the streets of Franklin with the passive innocence of a naked rear bumper. I was intimidated by lines of traffic with drivers who had found their political truth in the simple eloquence of a single letter. They were fortunate, in that they had escaped the vandalism of disapproval. I don't know if they had resisted the thought of leaving ugly residue, or having to get a sharp blade to remove the black-and-white keepsake of better times and public celebration. Sometimes cognitive dissonance outlasts reality, or the life of a bumper sticker.

I am not ready to commit my driver-side back bumper for four more years to extol the virtue and wisdom of some candidate who could either lose, or, even more tragic, win and embark upon a path of folly that might do irreparable harm to the security and quality of life of our country.

Indicative of our cultural and intellectual recession, bumper stickers and buttons seem less inspired and less poetic than those I displayed proudly when I was younger and more impressionable. Today's bumper stickers tend to be more angry and inconsistent with rational dialogue. Most of the messages now are inflammatory and divisive, combative and confrontational. Many are affirmations of faith; others are flagrant rejections or ridicule of someone else's faith.

We may have overdone the red circle and diagonal slash of disavowal. We have trivialized the meaning of life and choice beyond recognition. There may be nothing that hasn't been said about ecology, gun rights, global warming, abortion, intelligent design, prayer in public places, and 9/11. A year or two from now we may tire of first-name familiarity with Rudy, Fred, and Hillary, the ideological futility of Dennis Kucinich and Ron Paul, and sectarian political endorsements left and right. We can avoid the arrogance of flaunting victory, or the anger of losing.

It is not easy to find one simple phrase that defines your politics, your faith, your philosophy, your family values, and still expresses the passion and boundaries of your cultural and social activism. As one becomes more introspective and contemplative, one's thoughts become more complex and less adaptable to bumper-sticker simplicity. The words on bumper stickers are usually too few for meaningful comprehension, or too small to read at a safe distance, or too complex for the duration of one red light.

I looked for something related to my love of education, literacy, books, and children. I even found one that includes a statement of faith, values, and patriotism without being arrogant or condescending. If you are driving around Downtown Franklin or Cool Springs, look for a small sports car that has rejoined the road rhetoric with the statement, "War Leaves Every Child Behind." The time may come when I can remove this one, but not right now.

29

Article VI, No Religious Test

In the interpretation of our Constitution, we seem divided over strict construction or the idea of a document defined by prevailing culture. We try to assume from extraneous writings the intent of the framers to validate the phrasing of each mandate or prohibition.

In Article VI, section 3, we find, "…but no religious test shall ever be required as a qualification to any office or public trust under the United States." Thirteen years after the Constitutional Convention, Thomas Jefferson, a deist, was depicted by his opposition as an atheist. He was narrowly elected President by the House of Representatives, following a tie with Aaron Burr in electoral votes. Consistent with the election of 1800, we continue to impose religious tests in our elections of Presidents. In 2008, Mike Huckabee campaigned as the Christian candidate, while Mitt Romney felt compelled to defend his religious affiliation to solidify his support from conservative voters.

According to filtered Fox polls, 57% of those asked did not feel that voters would elect a Mormon for President. We overcame the misconception that a Catholic President would give priority to papal allegiance. One Muslim has been elected to Congress. Article VI binds elected officials by oath or affirmation, but it does not specify that the left hand be placed on the Bible, the Koran, or the Book of Mormon.

The Tennessee Constitution in Article I, section 4, repeats the same, almost verbatim. However, our state constitution disqualifies certain persons from holding public office in Article IX, section 1, which reads, "...no Minister of the Gospel, or priest of any denomination whatever, shall be eligible to a seat in either House of the Legislature." Section 2 reads, "No person who denies the being of God, or a future state of rewards and punishments, shall hold any office in the civil department of this State."

Some people believe that religious affiliation implies not only belief in a deity, but is also the source of moral and ethical behavior. Others would argue that doctrinal beliefs have no relevance to civil governance. We all agree that elected officials should make judgments based on moral and ethical values, whether derived from religious commands or secular interpretation.

This verbiage relates specifically to the holding of office or public trust, and does not relate to the elective process. Do we cast votes because a candidate is too religious or not religious enough? I see nothing in the Constitution that could negate the election, nor overturn the defeat, of any candidate whose election or defeat was the result of a real or perceived religious affiliation or doctrinal inclination.

Why would we make religion the focal point of the presidential debates? The Constitution is silent on partisan politics and does not control party primaries or conventions. Political parties function under party rules. If the Republicans should affirm that they would only nominate a conservative Christian, or if the Democrats should vow to nominate no person who publicly and officially supports the war in Iraq, neither is a violation of Article VI.

One might vote for or against someone who believes that civil rights begin at conception. One might choose a candidate who would favor reversal of the Supreme Court's decisions on First Amendment rights. The same decisions could apply to health care, gun rights, taxation, stewardship of the Earth, same-sex unions, and many other legislative and judicial decisions. These are talking points we often use to designate religious values, rightly or wrongly, as either conservative or liberal.

With respect to Article VI, unless something unforeseen happens between now and the next presidential election, I will probably vote for a candidate who is a Christian. With equal respect to constitutional law and my personal faith and politics, there is no religious test that the candidate must be a member of either the Conservative or Republican denomination of the Christian faith.

30

THE BEST OF TIMES, THE WORST OF TIMES

It was the best of times, it was the worst of times. With apologies to Charles Dickens, I would borrow from the despair of the French Revolution and the economic inequity of British industrialization to revisit a decade of despair in American history. A former American President suggested that if one believed that the Sixties was a good decade, he was likely to be a Democrat. If he believed the Sixties was a bad decade, he was more likely a Republican.

It was the age of wisdom, it was the age of foolishness. Our best and brightest on the campuses of American academia took over administration buildings and participated in sit-ins, marches, and freedom rides. The names Chaney, Goodman, and Schwerner will live forever, one Black and two Jewish boys who died in Mississippi.

It was the epoch of belief, it was the epoch of incredulity. The Byrds brought the biblical seasons of Ecclesiastes to a generation that had lost its faith in the church and organized religion. There was a time to every purpose under Heaven, but the generation that read us to sleep with Bible stories blocked the doors of schools, churches, and restaurants, denying access to some of God's children. A generation not remembered as the greatest was conscripted, killed, alienated, disillusioned, misled, and maligned.

Bill Peach

It was the season of light, it was the season of darkness. It was a time of the Kingston Trio, Joan Baez, of Peter, Paul and Mary, of jazz, of bluegrass, of Appalachian folk music. It was a time of marijuana and acid and Janis Joplin and Jimi Hendrix.

It was a season of fragile innocence, of protest and patriotism, a season for burning flags and crosses. It was a season of assassinations of JFK, MLK, and RFK, heroes remembered in the dramatic simplicity of three initials symbolic of the decade of peace and violence.

It was the spring of hope, it was the winter of despair. Congress passed the Voting Rights Act of 1965. We crossed the barrier of segregation in the universities of Mississippi and Alabama. We watched Buddhist monks douse themselves in gasoline and burn to death in the market squares of Vietnam. We watched Catholic priests be imprisoned for advocating resistance to war. Two and a half million Americans and Vietnamese died in a war that we came to decide was a mistake. My Lai and Kent State became symbols of infamy that would define the decade.

We had everything before us, we had nothing before us. We encountered Bull Conner, George Wallace, and Lester Maddox. The champions of segregation became the demagogic heroes of Southern politics. A death in Memphis changed the history of civil rights and integration. Thousands marched from Selma to Montgomery. We had 200,000 peaceful protesters in Washington, and riots in 110 cities. The poor and black of the inner cities bombed and burned the businesses and landmarks owned by the poor and black of the inner cities.

We were all going direct to Heaven, we were all going direct the other way. We stared in horror at the pictures of Vietnam, the naked nine-year-old girl running from the fireball of napalm, the graphic execution of the Viet Cong prisoner, and bloody and broken bodies of American sons and daughters, the screaming and pleading young woman caught up in the horror at Kent State, the soldier with a peace symbol and a cross on a chain around his neck framed by bandoleers of ammunition over his shoulders.

A generation advocating peace, love, justice, equality, and democracy lost confidence in and waged war against its government, its parents, its church. Four decades later, aging flower-children and heroic veterans have mingled their tears and shared their memories of the best of times and the worst of times, a time to weep, and a time to laugh, a time to keep silent, and a time to speak.

31

IDEOLOGUES, IDEALISTS, AND IDIOTS

Any organized system of beliefs, right or wrong, good or bad, held by any group or social class is called an ideology. That includes how a person or persons think, act, or interpret the world. There is nothing offensive about a generic definition of ideology. As we expand our vocabularies, we become more proficient in finding words to discredit persons without challenging their basic beliefs or intellectual skills, as in the pejorative *ideologue*.

If that belief system embraces aspirations of perfection and high standards, it is called idealism: still an ideology, but now obviously a noble one. Why, then, are practitioners and proponents of these belief systems called by names of disrespect?

If a person is fanatical in opposition to a belief system or political philosophy you support, you may use the word *ideologue* to reflect that fanaticism. In contrast, if a person is avid and outspoken in favor of your closely held views, you may not see him as a fanatic or condemn him as an ideologue. This would lead to interpreting the ideologue designation based not on someone's being zealous or doctrinaire, but rather on the espousal of a conflicting or erroneous ideology.

The prefixes *ideo-*, *idea-*, and *idio-* are barely distinguishable when spoken, causing much of the confusion. Idealism has a prominent place in philosophical dualism, but little value in normal conversation within that context. It applies, in normal dialogue, to the highest order of moral and ethical aspirations. This could be defined by many standards—holy Scripture, universally held moral principles, accepted excellence of demeanor, impeccable speech and cognitive skills. How, then, could an advocate of idealism, or an idealist, be held in disrespect?

Most idealists insist that perfection is an attainable goal. Realists insist that perfection is unattainable. Religious people insist that perfection is an attribute possessed only by deities, prophets, saints, and human or spiritual members of the Godhead. Believing that perfection is attainable usually leads one to reject practical considerations and eliminates compromise and tolerance.

Most ideologues and idealists, with their fanaticism and illusions, believe that their ideology and idealism are synonymous, and that conflicting ideas are untrue and imperfect. This is the general message of twenty-four-hour news channels, political debates, religious denominationalism, and staunch stands on social and economic issues. Wouldn't anyone embrace only idealistic ideologies, and reject ideologies that are inferior or antagonistic to that ideology?

Of lesser linguistic stature are words with the Greek root *idiotes*, from which we get such words as *idiot*, *idiocy*, and *idiotic*—all inappropriate, except possibly in a conversation between Al Franken and Rush Limbaugh. Not one of these words is appropriate for evaluations of mental illness, scholastic ineptitude, illogical reasoning, or absurdity of speech. Their only value is as weapons of choice in less-than-civil epithets between two persons of obvious inclusion.

The Greek and Indo-European origin of the prefix *idio-* is less offensive, meaning *self* or *private*. Very few words of this group do I find useful. The word *idiom* is useful relating to something unique in language, indigenous to that language or geographic area. I do like to use the word *idiosyncrasy* or *idiosyncratic* to identify peculiarities and persons who possess those peculiarities. Idiosyncratic people can be found among ideologues, idealists, and those of questionable intelligence.

The prefix *idio-* also carries the connotation of *proper* or *distinctive*, with some suggestion of elitism and qualitative uniqueness. Consequently, any idiosyncrasy is usually a conscious choice of persons who perceive themselves to be in some way distinctive. The same could be said about the ideologue and the idealist.

Those persons who take their place—at the podium, the dais, before the camera, on a panel, or in literary authorship—steeped in fanaticism, are usually easily identified. They come voicing a platform of perfection, sincerely believing that they uniquely personify some organized system of beliefs and values. When given a sufficient audience, and held to public scrutiny, and subjected to human evaluation, they may easily validate their rightful inclusion within any or all of these real or imagined designations.

32

WALL OF SEPARATION

The phrase Wall of Separation is not in the Constitution of the United States. As early as 1644, Roger Williams introduced the metaphorical term in calling for "a hedge or wall of separation between the garden of the church and the wilderness of the world." Most explanations of this confusion cite Jefferson's letter to the Danbury Baptists. The expression was repeated by Justice Hugo Black in a court decision in 1948: "both religion and government can best work to achieve their lofty aims if each is left free from the other within their respective sphere."

The framers of the Constitution struggled with the wording of the First Amendment to protect religion from governmental persecution. Those men of faith were convinced that all men should be free to worship whatever or however many God or gods they chose. That guarantee is clearly written in the Constitution.

Religious freedom included limiting government mandate of religious practices. The framers' intent was not to protect government from religion, but to protect freedom of religion from the tyranny of the state. Connecticut's Code of 1650 had included, "If any man shall have or worship any God but the Lord God, he shall be put to death." Virginia made it a crime to not have children baptized in the Anglican Church. Massachusetts limited suffrage and the right to hold office to members of the church. In Jamestown, those who failed to attend services twice daily would lose their food for the day. A second offense brought a whipping, and a third was punished by six months of incarceration. To miss church on Sunday, on the third offense, was a capital crime.

The First Amendment states that Congress shall make no laws respecting the establishment of religion. Can a government entity, at any level, even a school board, require or promote religious observation? Most judicial considerations cite the Fourteenth Amendment and the equal protection guarantee. Relating to school board jurisdiction, the 8 to 1 decision in *McCollum v. Board of Education* in 1948 is probably the clearest interpretation.

Lakeview Elementary School in Wilson County, Tennessee, has been the source of similar recent court cases, involving parental groups using school facilities and the intercom to promote church events and Bible study groups. The courts, at all levels, have defended student-initiated religious activity, but ruled against parental use of school facilities and school sponsorship of religious events.

Having grown up in a fundamentalist church, I understand the literal interpretation of biblical writings. I understand the emphasis on baptism, communion, and church attendance. I understand the right of any person to believe that certain acts of omission or commission are inconsistent with Scripture or other written sectarian or denominational creed.

Consider an actual exchange between two students in a cafeteria of a public elementary school in Wilson County. One student asks another student where she goes to church. Upon hearing an admission of her not attending any church, the first student avows that the non-attending student is going to Hell, then picks up her tray of food and moves to another table. At times, our sincere commitment to evangelism may overlook the innocence and vulnerability of children.

Thomas Jefferson insisted that civil authority could and should require certain protections and prohibit certain acts that inflict harm on another person. Civil law should not have the authority to mandate or prohibit religious ritual or practice unless such act violates the rights of others. Most importantly, the Founding Fathers believed that religion is a belief, protected under the inviolable freedom of thought.

If there is a wall separating one's personal spiritual beliefs about Nature's God, or lack thereof, from one's worth as a citizen in the public square, it should be torn down. The hedge, as a metaphorical boundary, defines the outermost limits of the church's careful plantings and establishes a barrier to the weeds and thistles of the wilderness, and also confines the sectarian blossoms. If there is no wall of separation between the institutional Church and the institutional State, at any and all levels of government, one should be built.

33

THE MIND AND SOUL OF AMERICA

Philosophy is mostly a collection of questions that may never be answered; religion is mostly a collection of answers that may never be questioned. Ideas with little or no obligation to fact or logic have the potential of robbing us of our innocence and crippling our hearts in the guise of expanding our minds.

I recently attended a gathering of area ministers at which we discussed, among other subjects, the real or imagined conflict or harmony between our history of scientific exploration in biological and physical sciences and our traditions of religious faith.

I want to understand the ethereality of the mind and soul within the physical human animal, having learned in a one-room church in southern Williamson County that we are created in the image of God. Less than a hundred feet from the church building, in a one-room school, grades one through eight, I found evidence that the cosmogony (or cosmology) of the heavens and the Earth did not fit neatly within the time frame and simplicity of the 31 verses of Genesis 1.

Within this inquiry, I think I see two possibilities. The universe either has always existed, or it came to be (or was created) at a finite time chronologically designated as its beginning.

I offer no verifiable scientific evidence to prove or disprove either. This continues to be discussed within the fields of philosophy and theology, and may be one of those questions that may never be answered.

This can be considered as philosophy or theology, or both, with differing levels of certainty or doubt. Existence requires no proof for validation. The origin of existence eludes explanation. Statements such as *we are, it is,* and *I am* (with a nod to Descartes) are innately accepted and undeniable. No learning is involved, no faith is required to know that we exist. Any discussion of the origin of existence without scientific verification may be either secular speculation or religious faith, or both.

How, then, do we approach this within the fields of natural sciences, in biology and physics, in botany and zoology? Scientific discovery includes a body of verifiable data, plus theories and hypotheses that drive the cycle of honest scientific inquiry. To the scientist, the ribbons of DNA, the human genome, immunology, stem-cell research, and the awesome senses of sight and hearing constantly expand the wonder of the mind. To the religious, to people of faith, to the theologian, scientific discovery brings logical evidence of the wonder of God. Who, then, could question the "intelligent" design of science?

The academic, or the intellectual, depending on definition, seeks a delicate harmony and separation of the mind and the soul. I use these words with some uncertainty, not to be confused with the physical function of the brain, or the metaphorical reference to the heart as the source and depository of emotion (*e.g.,* love, courage, compassion). We have come to envision and promote America as a nation in search of its mind and its soul, intellectually and spiritually.

We are a nation of many people. We have people of faith who have dedicated their lives to the acquisition of secular knowledge. We have intellectuals who ask the questions, secular and spiritual, to which we may never know the answers. We have theologians, ministers, people of the cloth, teachers of religion, who serve as custodians of the literal biblical narrative. We are a nation of people whose earliest ideas were shaped by nurturing teachers, in the classrooms and pews of our churches in matters of faith, and in our schools in matters of historical and scientific knowledge.

Dedicated to the search for the mind and soul of America, we should never in any forum or classroom impose on anyone an idea that would cripple the soul in the guise of expanding the mind, nor should we ever impose on anyone an idea that would cripple the mind in the guise of expanding the soul.

34

THE FALLACY OF FEAR

On the morning of Election Day November 2004, I was on a WAKM radio roundtable as the only Democrat among ten people. I made the statement that much of the political debate of the day would be between September 11th Americans and July 4th Americans. The moderator asked for an explanation for the radio audience. I don't think he believed or understood the implications of this differentiation.

The tragic events of September 11 changed our political attitudes and also changed the religious message coming from the Sunday morning American pulpit. Driven by love of country and moral outrage over acts of inhumanity, we accepted the President's appeal for national patriotism and his emotional dichotomy of being with us or with the terrorists. Over the ensuing seven years, September 11 became the partisan dialectical premise in a fallacy of fear. A nation that was already divided politically and spiritually, found new battle lines for our intramural war. The voices of fear became the framers of foreign policy and national security. Fear and emotion thrive with a greater visual and audible media presence. Logic and rationality are often lost in unspoken contemplation.

These voices of fear can come from both the political and the religious alarmists. There is a parallel. There are those in the religious community who speak of End Times, of the Rapture, of Left Behind literature, of Armageddon. Some would politically equate this with America's role in a predestined unfolding of Apocalyptic history, and of God's wrath in our tragedies and God's approval in our successes. They speak of a manifest destiny for America to overthrow evil dictators, establish democracies, and build nations. They speak of evil, of extremism, of insurgency, of suicide bombers, of border security, of secularists, of a unified attack on America and on God and on all things good. The voices of fear interpret dissent as blasphemy against an ordained supremacy of the Presidency.

The July 4th group has been slow in making its voice heard. It speaks of a Constitution and the vision and wisdom in the writings of the Founding Fathers. It speaks of the First Amendment and the freedoms of speech and print and assembly and redress of grievance and of religion. It speaks of free will and secular intellect, of tolerance, of compassion, of diversity, of diplomacy, and our role in the community of nations. These are usually spoken in abstraction, often lost in an ambiguous monolith of nationalism, capitalism, democracy, Judeo-Christian heritage, and the diplomacy of a strong military.

Since the fiery fall of the World Trade Center towers, both our politics and our religion have been driven almost entirely by fear. There is the fear of chemical, bacteriological, and nuclear weapons of mass destruction used on American cities. We are afraid of the fire and brimstone of Hell. We are afraid of the images of bearded terrorists, who engender sectarian hatred and acts of sacrificial homicide. As we circled our wagons of defense, we became afraid of dissent, of thinking a different thought, of walking a lesser-trodden path.

I have just injected into this writing my own fallacy of fear. I am appealing to your fear, not to your rationality and intellect.

I don't know that I could ever explain the content and basic structure of the belief system of July 4th Americans. It has not been effectively articulated, and is most often dismissed as irrelevant by those who do not embrace it. The result has been a bilateral accusation of the lesser or greater threat to our freedoms.

Fear has become the most effective device in the peaceful and elective transition of power within a democracy. It can either perpetuate and retain a government empowered by fear, or it can incite an electorate which has become frightened of such a government. That electorate, driven by that fear, may eventually elect a voice of reason that can refute the fallacy and end the cycle of governance by fear.

35

THE UN-CHURCHED AND THE OVER-CHURCHED

For the past year, I have been visiting different churches in the area on Sunday mornings. My earliest religious experiences in a rural church environment gave me little exposure to religious diversity. A doctrinal wall of separation between Methodists and Baptists and Catholics divided a town along lines that now seem so illogical to me. On one recent visit, I shared a worship service with a congregation that is truly multi-cultural and multi-ethnic. Having lived here seventy-one years, I have watched the climate of racial harmony change more easily in the secular community than in the religious community. Historically, we have been painfully divided on Sunday mornings along lines of cultural and doctrinal differences.

My itinerary has included seven Churches of Christ. Five were white and two black, a Sunday morning separation perpetuated by tradition and community, irrelevant in the sincerity of hugs and handshakes. I visited mainstream Episcopal, Presbyterian, and Baptist churches. I met with several newer groups designated as Community churches, a more meaningful cohesion than many doctrinal bonds. I was also warmly welcomed at a Catholic church and a Church of Latter-Day Saints. I revisited two of my favorite liberal congregations in Nashville. So far, I have found very few liberal churches in

Williamson County. If you know of one, let me know. I have found some liberal clergy who serve politically and socially conservative churches.

Some people who move here are fortunate to find a minister and fellowship similar to the church they had to leave when they moved. Families with children feel the need to raise children in a church environment. The church becomes the welcoming home for community involvement.

Established churches that recruit the un-churched risk alienating their traditional membership. Churches that resist change do not grow numerically. Consequently, contemporary start-up churches have been more proficient in attracting the nontraditional.

New inter- or nondenominational churches present a calculated appeal to the un-churched and the over-churched. From my background in the Church of Christ, I understand both. I understand the attraction for a younger, exciting, visually emotional style of worship. From my humanistic moorings, I also understand the move from dogma to a more rational theology.

Organized spirituality within a church configuration usually touches the total person of its members. To feel comfortable in this setting, each person can select from a menu of participation in worship, activism, benevolence, fellowship, education, and the mundane physical and fiscal needs of an earthbound brick-and-mortar church. How, then, does one find and join a church or congregation with the greatest level of commonality?

At Strong Tower Bible Church, I was welcomed by a warm and loving church, before and after the praise and worship period. As the music began, I looked around the assembly for demographic indicators. The audience was young and old; it was dressed in Sunday finery and tattered denim.

The music was performed by the church choir and a talented group of musicians. By all standards of contemporary Christian music, it was excellent, I think. As the excitement of the worshipers evoked clapping and rhythmic movement, arms lifted and waving, I witnessed the success of a new Christianity that I did not understand. I saw the excitement of the previously un-churched. I saw the spirit-filled worship of the over-churched who had escaped a former life in an unemotional, ritualistic, maybe dogmatic, maybe unfriendly, inherited church of their parentage. The magic of contemporary praise and worship was irrelevant to me, and I felt that I was a spectator, not a participant. For me, praise and worship is a quiet, contemplative relationship with God.

I spent a few minutes with the pastor. Normally I do not speak highly of the clergy categorically, but I do find some spiritual giants among them. This pastor and his church family have helped build an amazing cultural and theological harmony in our community.

After the praise and worship service, I stayed and watched a movie, *Amazing Grace*, based on the life of William Wilberforce, an Englishman who dedicated his life to the abolition of the slave trade in England. I could sense the horrific smell of death of the human cargo on the slave ships. I watched a devout man wrestle with the difficult choice between the pulpit or the House of Commons. As I watched the final vote passing his resolution, tears ran down my cheeks. It is possible for the un-churched and the over-churched to commune in one place in the presence of God.

36

The Naked Lapel

The buttonhole in the lapel of a man's suit is a nonfunctional vestige from the days when coats were buttoned at the neck for warmth. More recently, it has become a wedge issue for personal political ridicule.

Much of my experience with lapel pins came during my membership in the Jaycees and later in the Rotary Club. I wore both pins proudly, not all the time, usually at events or meetings of either. Lapels pins are seen as unspoken soliloquies proclaiming who we are and what we believe. The most frequently seen are American flags for patriotism and either a cross or a fish for religious affirmation.

I have resisted the urge to wear either a flag or cross on my lapel for several reasons. A lapel pin has the potential for initiating a confrontational conversation, or the viewer may make a hasty assumption that your symbolic display of patriotism or spirituality coincides with his or her definition of those virtues.

Years ago, a manufacturer's representative, making a sales call with me, came into our store wearing a lapel pin that was a gold replica of two tiny feet, the size of those of an unborn at a specific stage of fetal development. One of the television evangelists had sold these for a love offering to support his ministry. I admired the salesman for his courage to risk his commission earnings in expressing his sincere reverence for life. I could feel the passion in his heart, but I kept seeing the face of a religious demagogue preying upon the fragility of innocence and sincerity. I am concerned that we have allowed preachers and politicians to usurp ownership of the buttonhole to divide our nation.

I am also guilty of using the apparel arts as a platform of opinion. I own seven ties with literary images. My favorite middle daughter gave me one that she found at a gift shop, and I ordered six other styles, including one with a Shakespearean theme. I wear one almost every day. It helps promote reading, creative writing, and occasionally gives me an opportunity to sell one of my books. Almost every day I am blessed with a conversation with someone who finds pleasure in books and education.

Recently, on a visit to a doctor's office, I did not wear a tie. After I left my house, I had a frightening thought. What if someone sees me not wearing a tie with books on it and wonders if I have lost my love for reading and literature and my support for the literary community?

I don't own any ties with flags or crosses. Some people do. I do have one tie with flags and donkeys, but that is more of an esoteric tie. I wear it mostly for political gatherings. Actually, I wear the tie to confuse Republicans, many of whom believe that flags and donkeys are in some way mutually exclusive symbols.

The cross and the fish, our iconic symbols of Christianity, seem to have relinquished their position in buttonhole advocacy and moved to a more prominent presence in jewelry and bumper stickers. We should be reluctant to be judgmental. One person's icon of sincere expression of spiritual advocacy may be seen to the skeptic as a trinket of vanity or philosophical ostentation.

The controversy now seems to be focused on the flag pin, or the absence thereof, as a mechanism of political posturing. We are asked to judge our candidates for President by whether or not they are wearing a flag on their lapel. The irony, or fallacy, of symbolic iconography is that when we assign a virtue or evil to a graven ornament, we equally distort the meaning of an unadorned lapel. I don't know that wearing a symbol on one's person accurately interprets the content of the heart. We may have taken superficiality to a new depth.

37

Misspeaking and Misthinking

Politicians and media personalities who spend their time in front of cameras and microphones are often brought before the altar of human condemnation begging forgiveness for having misspoken. Barack Obama, for example, during the 2008 primaries, misspoke in California regarding a segment of the population who, in anger and bitterness, embraced their religion and their guns. Public outcry voiced a natural offense that he had implied that religion and the Second Amendment were refuge for the frightened and the angry.

Weeks later, Mike Huckabee, speaking at a meeting of the National Rifle Association, injected a misdirected joke at Barack Obama. He reacted to an offstage noise identifying it as Obama tripping over a chair, distracted that someone had pointed a gun at him. The remark played well at the NRA gathering, but incited a cry for apology once aired in the Blue State parts of America. I am a little concerned when a former minister/governor jokes about someone being afraid of a gun. Considering the acerbic tone of the campaign, one could be concerned that the clear-and-present-danger boundary of freedom of speech may have been crossed. Huckabee was wise to issue an apology.

Not having learned from widely publicized inappropriate

Politics, Preaching & Philosophy

remarks, the Tennessee Republican Party launched a television advertisement aimed at Michelle Obama. The focus of the ad was her ambiguous reference to the first time in her adult life she had been proud of her country, another example of sound-bite vulnerability. However, the advertisement was poorly conceived and artistically tasteless. The images included a Vanderbilt graduate student whose message was unclear, followed by a video of a man shooting pool in a recreation room or den, with a background of rifles and shotguns mounted on the wall. This was well planned to appeal to a voter base. In a vernacular that would bring an English teacher to tears, the man avows his inalienable right to bear arms and to worship God wherever and whenever he pleases.

As a defender of our inalienable Bill of Rights, I wish our state Republicans had not linked the First and Second Amendments within a political message that some may find offensive. Such an associative equation tended to trivialize religion and attach some spiritual implication to the right to bear arms.

I offer two other meaningful quotes. There is a hymn from my early Church of Christ days that opens, "Angry words—oh, let them never from the tongue unbridled slip. May the heart's best impulse ever check them ere they soil the lip." The other quote is from a Sixties-era comedian, Dave Gardner. When asked if he had to watch what he said, he answered, "No, I just have to watch what I think."

We have an oft-used word, *misspeak*, to identify the inarticulate sin of incorrect and inappropriate speech, but my dictionaries disavow the usage of misthink as being archaic. Since we cannot know the unspoken thoughts of our candidates, we judge the content of their hearts based upon our interpretation of their spoken words. Compassion for human frailty demands that we forgive the lingual ineptitude of the penitent.

Errors of speech, innocent or malicious, are easily detected and quickly corrected by apology or disclaimer, or consensual media lynching.

It is easy to chastise our politicians for errors of speech. Their every word is replayed in prime time. Errors of speech are condemned in the public forum and ultimately judged on lack of merit or truth. God, in His wisdom, gave us the right of quietude and privacy within the human mind. Unspoken thoughts go unquestioned. The great advances and tragedies of human history have originated, rightly or wrongly, within the realm of human thought. Words, spoken and misspoken, then, become our windows to detect the subliminal indicators of lingual clumsiness or the blatant defamation of political villainy.

38

Ego, Elitism, and Excellence

The elimination of ancestry as a valid determinant of comparative human value is the keynote of any democracy. Designations of blue-blood nobility and inherited patrician superiority were theoretically precluded in all of our founding documents of governance. Consequently, in America, being a member of an elite class has no methodology for official perpetuation of advantage of birth. Public disapproval of all concepts of elitism has given voice to a new group of people who have found social advantage in the gift of humble birth.

This should not correlate with disapproval of any substantive skills and accomplishments upon which we have come to define the superlative or preferable attributes of excellence. In our commitment to democracy and equality, we may have confused the concept of constitutional equality with an unlikely and undesirable society of uniformity and mediocrity. In any culture, there have been, and will continue to be, those who become leaders by their labor, education, capital, or other element of good fortune. Rightfully, we have referred to these persons with words of approval that validate some tangible superiority based on accomplishment rather than the benefit of birth.

In contrast, elitism is usually defined as snobbery, hubris, and aloofness. Most people assign a higher level of importance to attributes and images in which they think they excel, aspire to, or avow inclusion. The accepted requisites of elitism are most often measured in physical attractiveness, artistic skill, education, or wealth. Earned wealth and fame derived from innate and enhanced artistic talent and physical skills may rightfully transcend the perception of non-substantive elitism.

An accomplished songwriter and famous personality once told me, "I can admit to being good as long as I never forget that it is a gift." From this I learned two things. Accept without false humility whatever praise might come your way for your accomplishments based on that gift. Secondly, avoid media and public scrutiny of your participation or competition in areas in which you have limited gifts and competitive disadvantage.

In the field of education we are obligated to encourage, educate, and empower students toward excellence in every aspect of human development—academia, social skills, morality, and wellness. As we do this, students develop self-esteem at all levels, from serving as class president, earning top grades, enjoying athletic prowess, to succeeding at incremental skills despite special needs. We demand academic excellence, and accept with love and encouragement the attainment of something slightly less.

How, then, does this evolve and translate into responsible adulthood and realistic self-esteem? There is an old truism and guideline for recognition that says, "It is better that people wonder why nobody ever erected a monument in your honor, than to wonder why somebody did."

Elitism tends to promote a counter-culture of anti-elitism, which often becomes a reactionary form of elitism. For example, we analyze our political and consumer preferences on demographic data of age, income, gender, education, or religious affiliation. Pollsters often suggest predictability of NASCAR fans who shop at Wal-Mart, who attend church twice a week, own a gun, and are hard-working blue-collar Americans. Do we really elect our public officials, choose our clothing designers, follow our spiritual gurus, read our bestsellers, and drive Volvos to Starbucks in a benign herdlike defiance of logic and individuality?

All of us disavow the implied and predictable inseparability of our demographic factors of ethnicity, gender, age, and education in shaping personal preferences in pastors, politics, sports, music, and consumer products. Most people see elitism as a self-defined societal inclusion and exclusion arrived at by a series of choices rather than realities of success and failure.

Elitism should never be flaunted publicly in first-person exhibitionism. Praise and public adoration bestowed by others are more acceptable measures of human accomplishment, though not necessarily more accurate. I do believe we should be governed, inspired, and shepherded by an elite few. We just need a better standard of excellence for selection.

39

ROTC, Recruiters, and Resisters

I was told at Middle Tennessee State University, a land grant college, that all males were required to take ROTC their first two years. I endured the parade and polish for two weeks until someone told me that students who transfer in as a sophomore are not required to take ROTC.

That was fall semester of 1957, long before the Vietnam War, long before our occupation of Iraq. I would never question the morality or patriotism of the World War II heroes, and I respect my college peers enrolled in the ROTC program. My uncertain aversion to the military existed long before I entered the politics of opposition to ill-chosen wars. There was something about collateral destruction of life and home that was intrinsically incongruous with my Christian upbringing.

My exemption from ROTC, my college deferment for three years, and six years in the Army Reserve from 1960 to 1966 enabled me to avoid the dreaded draft during the Vietnam War. I have mixed feelings about an all-volunteer military. I don't know if we can sustain a viable military without a draft. Given the combative mood of our recent political leadership, our citizenry probably would not tolerate a draft. When a majority of our population believes that the invasion of Iraq was a mistake, the burden of fighting this war falls on volunteer patriots who are deployed to combat a second and third time.

Without a draft, we are dependent on voluntary enlistments. We have to convey two important messages. We have to protect the heroic and noble image of military service, and secondly, we have to financially reward our best and brightest with fair remuneration for choosing a military career.

We who openly and loudly oppose specific wars are often accused of disloyalty and disrespect for those who choose to serve. I was fortunate to have worn the uniform of our Army. I felt the pain of the country's anger over Vietnam from both sides.

How, then, does an aging flower-child and veteran see the role of military service at a time when we are fighting another war, with the same mistakes, the same questions, and the same deception at the highest level of government? God blessed me with three daughters, none of whom expressed any interest in military service. I resist frequent temptation to impose my philosophy on grandchildren. They are bombarded by simulated computer war-games, a cannon on every street corner, and monuments and memorials to fallen heroes. They applaud the glowing skies of Shock and Awe, the arrest and execution of Saddam Hussein, and share our hatred for terrorism and weapons of mass destruction in the hands of rogue nations.

As a member of the school board, I cannot question the decisions of students or parents who choose Junior ROTC as a high school course or who meet with on-campus recruiters. I wish I could have a table beside the recruiters and tell the students what a future in the military is like. I realize our children watch television coverage of small Iraqi children lined against the wall of their home as our military knocks down their front door. They see isolated acts of inhumanity from both sides. They know the statistics on suicides and divorces of our military. They see husbands and wives, mothers and fathers, being away from small children for multiple deployments, even as Reservists. They counted with us as the number of military fatalities grew beyond four thousand, with the loss of limbs and sight and normal body functions growing daily

Those of us who serve on boards of education take our role seriously. One could argue that our responsibility is limited to academics and discipline. We like to believe that there is more. Our counselors and advisors are involved in choices of class offerings, graduation rates, college admission, and eventually career choices and quality of life. However, we respect the role of parents, and must painfully remain silent in the most life-changing decisions in the lives of their children.

40

Liberation Theology

This phrase was brought to our attention recently by some inflammatory words spoken by Jeremiah Wright from the pulpit of Trinity United Church of Christ in Chicago. I dismissed him as an arrogant, egotistical charlatan of the cloth not too different from the myriad of screaming practitioners of deception that we see in the mega-churches of cable television.

His first offense was his bombastic and flagrant complicity with those who seek to impugn the spirituality, patriotism, and integrity of Barack Obama. The greater offense was his defamation of the image of the United Church of Christ and on the historical integrity of liberation theology. The theology of liberation is more accurately defined by the work of the Catholic Church and Archbishop Oscar Romero in Central America, particularly in Nicaragua and El Salvador. Activism was prevalent among the clergy from their belief that Christian churches have a duty to oppose social, economic, and political oppression of the disenfranchised.

During the period between 1960 and 1985, the awkward interaction of Christian missions in Central America and the Communist resistance to government led to the torture, expulsion, and assassination of Catholic priests, including Romero.

In 1979, the priests were caught in the junta that overthrew the government of El Salvador during a wave of human rights abuses by the government-supported right-wing paramilitary forces. Archbishop Romero wrote and warned President Jimmy Carter that continued U.S. military aid would "undoubtedly sharpen the injustice and the repression inflicted on the organized people, whose struggle has often been for respect for their most basic human rights."

At the same time, a similar paradox was occurring in America. The involvement of Catholic, liberal, and African-American churches in the civil-rights and anti-war movements intensified the left/right divide within our churches and our politics. Christians who openly opposed the Vietnam War or segregation were often labeled as leftist-leaning during a time of anti-Communist paranoia.

Trinity United Church of Christ was established in 1961 by twelve middle-class black families who had moved from a low-income South Side of Chicago. They initially met in the gymnasium of a Chicago elementary school. Its members marched and supported civil rights efforts in the Sixties. A later effort to merge with a white congregation fell through over resistance to integration. The church opposed black militancy and influence of the Nation of Islam and the Black Hebrew Israelites at a time when many blacks were leaving Christianity. It was within this context that their pastor, Reverend Reuben Sheares, adopted the motto "Unashamedly Black and Unapologetically Christian" to send the message that Christianity was not just a religion for white people.

Jeremiah Wright took Trinity to a more radical black-liberation theology, leading to the loss of many members to a local Pentecostal Apostolic church. The national leadership of UCC tried to distance itself from Wright, but later reached a level of reconciliation.

Why did a man with the obvious human compassion and intellect of Barack Obama sit in the pews of Trinity UCC for twenty years? Why did I spend my young adult life in the pews of Church of Christ congregations that resisted fellowship with black Christians? Why did John McCain, a man of faith and moderate social views, find himself within the favor and endorsement of the radical voices of pastors whose words show no compassion or spiritual tolerance?

The mission of Christians to minister to "the least of these" has often brought us into conflict between populist activism and the oppression of political tyranny and theological orthodoxy. We asked, What was the role of the black church in segregated inner-city slums of Northern migration and the sharecropper hopelessness of Southern anachronism? We asked, What was the role of the Catholic Church in the struggle for freedom in El Salvador and Nicaragua? It was violent reaction to liberation theology that took the life of a Baptist preacher in Memphis and a Catholic archbishop whose blood actually spilled on his church altar moments after his completing a prayer in preparation for the Eucharist.

41

Controversy, Consensus, and Compromise

One of the frailties of controversy is that it thrives in the minds and voices of a few. If, or when, a minority opinion attracts the support of the majority, it loses its underdog status and is no longer controversial. Consensus, with or without verity or logic, usually has the benefit of tradition and the obvious numerical advantage. The word *consensus* may or may not imply unanimity, but demands general agreement without debate or argument.

I grew up in an environment of consensus. Our only church was Bible based, and any doctrinal differences were assigned to someone else and dismissed as false doctrine. Our only school had all eight grades taught by one teacher, whose knowledge was validated by state-adopted textbooks. Our only retail outlet, a country store, was a forum for like-minded farmers educated by like-minded ancestry. Our polling-place voter registration list included only two Republicans, whom we dismissed from relevance by an unexplained reference to the depression and Herbert Hoover. We accepted the rationing of sugar and gasoline; we did without new cars, new tires, and new clothes to support World War II. Our sons, brothers, fathers, and uncles were all heroes. The Allies were the good guys; the Axis was or were the bad guys.

I find greater comfort in controversy than in consensus. We hear references to moral majorities or silent majorities depicting implied consensus, which is fine, except it may give non-substantive status to those whose inclusion is validated only by silence. My religious background drew me to the Church of Christ at Fourth Avenue in Franklin. It had that combination of historical integrity and a membership that included an inner circle of business and community leaders. Theologically I was part of consensus as I saw it. In time I came to understand that my steeple of choice was not only a minority within the community, but by its intrinsic fundamentalism was controversial.

In my recent visits to many churches, I have found very little controversy in religion, but an uncertainty in consensus. This has been achieved by a shift from theological discourse to an emphasis on praise and worship. Such a shift has enabled Christian churches to unite through compromise without the requisite of consensus. For example, I have not been denied Holy Communion at any Protestant church. The consensus is a simple inclusion within the discipleship of Jesus, and faith in God. The weighty issues of Heaven or Hell, determining whether one was saved or lost, that I had been taught all my life, have been replaced by menu-driven choices of taste and preference.

How, then, and why is there, or can there be, controversy in religion? At one recent Sunday morning assembly, the pulpit lesson was an academic expository, without advocacy, of three different ideas related to millennialism. The membership, comfortable with the pulpit philosophy and trust in the minister, found comfort in the consensus of an obvious rejection of an illogical doctrine.

Denominations have learned to avoid controversy. We do this by either accepting differences of religious interpretation as insignificant and non-divisive, or better yet, we stay away from each other. Sunday mornings provide a great sociological spiritual experience. We give names to our churches and put signs on the buildings; we hire musicians and preachers; we market our image to the potential flock. After several visits, families find the combination of worship, youth activity, Bible study, charity, and activism to their liking and become part of a supportive consensus of inclusion.

Monday through Saturday, in the daily discourse of politics, social philosophy, human rights, and other secular subjects, we may separate the secular from the spiritual, leaving our theology at the church door. Or we may, in the evangelical tradition, embrace and proclaim our Sunday's sermon as a singular source of truth equally binding also on those who have chosen to attend their respective houses of worship. As the ultimate compromise, we have to accept that there are others who search for truth outside the walls of consensus.

42

THE UNLIKELY RESOLUTION OF LIFE AND CHOICE

In the best of all worlds, all sexual acts would be consensual; all pregnancies would be wanted; all babies would be born sound of mind and body; and all children would be loved and nourished in a two-parent upper-middle-class home in Williamson County.

Historically, the debate over the legality or criminality of abortion has been primarily between persons who believe that an embryo or fetus has legal status as a citizen, which overrides a pregnant woman's option to terminate an unwanted or unintended pregnancy, and those who believe in a woman's right to terminate a pregnancy.

We have overlooked the statistics of abortions and the medical community's effort to save the victims of 600,000 abortions performed illegally. When we defend or seek to overturn *Roe v. Wade*, we forget that decision was rendered by nine conservative old men by a vote of 7 to 2. If we limit or overturn *Roe v. Wade*, abortions will again be done—covertly, illegally, and dangerously—in backrooms and secret places. Abortion will again become not just emotionally agonizing, but a life-threatening decision for thousands of young women, many of whom will die. When you read the statistics on deaths during the time when abortions were illegal, the terms *pro-life* and *pro-choice* seem to have little meaning.

Some portray the reproductive-rights issue as a battle between Christians and non-Christians; between the religious and the secular; between those who oppose abortion and those who support abortion; between those who believe in the sanctity of life and those who have no regard for human life. If this were true—if this were a political or theological absolute—the debate would have ended long before *Roe v. Wade*.

During the 2004 and 2008 election cycles, many states offered amendments or initiatives that would limit reproductive rights. The logistics of this was to pass a resolution, but also to attract a voter base that would elect a President and senators who would appoint and confirm two or more Supreme Court Justices who would shift the balance of political power on the Court to eventually limit or overturn *Roe v. Wade*.

We hear the unfortunate pejorative *pro-birth* which critics on the left repeat to discredit the label *pro-life*. On the other side of this elusive dialogue, from the right, is the pejorative *pro-abortion* to discredit the term *pro-choice*. This continues to stifle rational discussion, in that the designations *pro-life* and *pro-choice* have become political invectives to promote fear in the elective process. These terms are used only within the discussion of abortion or reproductive rights, depending on one's bias, and are rarely expanded for valid application to universal views on the sanctity of life or matters of choice in the full interpretation of constitutional rights.

Some people believe that life, with full constitutional rights, begins at conception. Any termination of a pregnancy by chemical, surgical, or whatever means, is the equivalent of murder and a violation of the human right of the unborn. Others believe that life is an unbroken continuity within the laws of God or Nature or both, and that constitutional rights are bestowed at birth, and are inherent in a woman's most personal and difficult decisions.

The political conflict to determine the electoral balance of

Red States and Blue States will continue to be fought state by state. Our revolutionary advocates avowed that we are endowed with certain inalienable rights. Historically, we have found that in the pursuit of individual happiness, one person's life and liberty may be contingent upon restraining the behavior of another or defining the collective conscience of the community. Is abortion murder and an abomination before God? Is abortion a woman's inalienable constitutional right? Regardless of who sits in the White House or controls the Senate, regardless of appointments and the resultant balance of the Supreme Court, this will continue to be discussed by groups with diametric views that each considers to be absolute.

43

THE FIRST AND SECOND AMENDMENTS

If you were asked to pick ten basic rights to include as amendments to our original Constitution, which would you choose? The debate between the Federalists and the Democratic-Republicans included whether or not specific rights should be enumerated in the Constitution, and if so, which rights. Several of the states expressed a desire to add certain restrictive clauses to prevent misconstruction and abuse of power to best ensure the beneficence of its existence. James Mason refused to sign the Constitution and opposed its ratification without these guarantees.

In the last two sessions of the Supreme Court, approximately one-fourth of the cases brought before the Court were decided by 5 to 4 votes. Many of these close decisions were interpretations of the intent of the founders relating to our First and Second Amendments. The First Amendment is complex in its opposition of establishment of religion and its guarantee of free exercise. This complexity has perpetuated the great divide between the theocrats and the secular separatists. The Second Amendment, with its opening and ambiguous reference to a well regulated militia, followed by the assurance that the right to bear arms shall not be infringed, ensures an endless debate between advocates of gun rights and gun control.

There is in both of these debates conflict between law, logic, and emotional attachment to a common practice or principle. When you ask a Liberal about priority, the answer comes back as an emotional affinity for the First Amendment, rarely with any reference to the Second. Most Conservatives seeking elected public office will avow support for the Second Amendment, adding that the often-misinterpreted First Amendment is protected by the rights guaranteed in the Second Amendment.

The polarities have become emotional. Conservatives embrace the free-exercise clause of the First Amendment and the "shall not be infringed" clause of the Second Amendment. Liberals embrace "shall make no law respecting an establishment of religion" and "well regulated militia" to further inflame the debate. Each side fears and warns against the slippery-slope principle. Those who believe we are a Christian nation, and that our laws are derived from religion, fear any restraint of government-sanctioned religious activity. The terms *gun rights* and *gun control* have become the left/right battle lines of legislative or judicial interpretation of the Second Amendment.

I don't fully understand the parallel between gun ownership and religion. When you listen to talk radio, you will hear an implied correlation between gun ownership and advocacy of religion in public places and government meetings.

We all agree that a firearm is an inanimate object. As we say, guns don't kill people, people do. I think the 2008 Supreme Court decision overturning the District of Columbia ban is probably the proper interpretation. In 1787, one would assume that most of our four-million population owned a firearm, if for no other reason than food for the table, not to mention threats from wild animals and roving outlaws. The reference to and the need for the militia had more relevance then than it might now. The Court acknowledged the right of local jurisdiction in matters of registration, background checks, type of weapon, and public safety.

In today's cultural and political debate, some people believe that ownership and possession of a firearm is a constitutional right that protects the law-abiding citizen, reduces crime, and is beneficial to public safety. Those persons are more likely hunters or sportsmen. Other people believe that firearms are a danger to public safety. They fear the presence of guns in retail establishments and other public gatherings. Those persons are probably not hunters or sportsmen. There is continuing fear that our government will outlaw and confiscate all firearms and Bibles, and a counter-fear of the political clout of the National Rifle Association and the Religious Right. Herein lies an almost equal divide in two of the most vocal and emotional issues of our culture.

44

The Age of Evangelical Enlightenment

The history of civilization is written in revolution, sometimes violent, sometimes philosophical. The struggle between change and establishment came with many names. We refer to the Age of Enlightenment, the Age of Reason, Reformation, Renaissance, the Great Awakening, Humanism, and in our more recent pop culture, the Age of Aquarius. Those of us who consider ourselves people of faith find it awkwardly offensive that most of these periods have been depicted as conflicts between religion and intellect, or between religious orthodoxy and tolerance of diversity.

In the earliest writings of Church history, there were warnings against those who would teach or practice blasphemy or deviance from the Word of God. In the next few centuries, established religion, as the Holy Roman Empire, was transformed into an authoritarian entity, tyrannical and corrupt. From this configuration of papal and imperial dominance, a long tradition of conflict between religious establishment and the voices of reason defined the lines between religion and the cyclical emergence of secular enlightenment. We may be in a yet-to-be-named period in history, in this continuing conflict between religions, that involves very little change in doctrinal disputes and the participants.

In April of 2008, I began a series of church visitations, hearing different preachers, in different churches, in different denominations or nondenominational bodies. From this limited sampling, I would not try to write a definitive analysis of contemporary religion. The brevity of Sunday morning fellowship in praise and worship does not convey the full narrative of theology. I do not know why people choose a specific denomination and congregation within that denomination. From my spectator vantage point, I can't interpret decisions based on statements I hear from church members.

Obviously, cultural and social commonalities outweigh location. I found an interesting resurgence of both commonality and diversity. The churches that are growing fastest seem to be the ones that are most Bible centered. My early history in the Church of Christ was defined by a body of laws and examples that were essential for salvation and Sunday morning worship. In contrast, I find contemporary religious inclusion to be a submission to a narrative of divine purpose, with little demand for doctrinal uniformity. Individuals seem to find solace within a congregation rather than any allegiance to a denomination. There is also an inverse preference for small community churches and churches with a multi-thousand memberships. Factors that attract the many will probably repel the few.

My church music was a hymn led by a self-taught *a cappella* song leader. Physical manifestation of spiritual praise and worship I still associate with early images of Pentecostal tent-revivalism of a rural South. Growing up in rural Williamson County, I did not participate in the sartorial competition between Presbyterians and Episcopalians. Having become a men's clothing consultant, I am equally unimpressed by the calculated the beleaguered denim and rumpled cotton from Abercrombie & Fitch and American Eagle. The prevailing irony for me is that the Sunday morning period that we call praise and worship has almost no relevance to my theology. A Presbyterian apologized to me because their choir had taken a summer respite. Inside these different houses of worship, I found no less or greater divine presence than in the serenity of a coffee shop, a classroom, a board meeting, or the conversation of kindred minds on a busy street corner, or the solitude of back-porch meditation.

Members of these friendly and welcoming congregations asked if I had found a church that I liked and would like to join. The simple answers, which I could not explain, are sequentially, yes and no. I don't know how to tell them I am not shopping, I am learning. I cannot write with any clarity about the mind and soul of the South without sitting in its culturally diverse pews. I do not come to be taught. I come to learn.

Much of the history of enlightenment has been shaped by intellectuals who filled the pulpits of our churches. Sometimes enlightenment needs some light from outside sectarian walls to find its truth.

45

A GENERATION OF PHILOSOPHERS

Long before I became a published writer, I was introduced by Tom T. Hall as a philosopher to an audience at the Southern Festival of Books. This may have been the first time I had heard the word as a personal reference other than in jest or derision. One of the several definitions of *philosopher* is "somebody who believes in a particular philosophy and thinks and acts accordingly." That could be anybody. My claim or accusation came primarily from my laborious and circuitous analysis of spiritual and secular questions that most Williamson County scholars had either filed in their folder as too obvious for inquiry or rejected as blasphemy or absurdity.

I like the definition "a thinker who deeply and seriously considers human affairs and life in general." The depth and seriousness does not have to equate that of the great thinkers whose writings and utterances we teach within the academic subject we call Philosophy. However, the word *philosopher* suggests some gravity beyond merely holding and expressing an opinion, more likely based on personal judgment rather than serious examination.

In its Greek etymology it translates as "lover of knowledge, learning, or wisdom." This is the common theme on which we all agree. Except, one person's toolbox of knowledge may not contain a blueprint for wisdom, and another's wisdom may be without practical application. We have an inclination to be lovers of our own wisdom more than the wisdom of someone else with whom we might not agree.

The most ambiguous definition is one of attitude and demeanor, a person who "calmly and rationally reacts to events, especially adversity." Often the calm and rational person who does not react or respond emotionally and definitively may not be invited back to the roundtable of confrontation.

In the field of academia, within the department of Philosophy, one would find a limited list of course offerings. These would include variations of five basic fields of philosophy, plus the principles and history of thought and the writings and influence of those persons whom we have designated as the great philosophers of world cultures. The bad news is that there are few elected or ordained career opportunities for philosophy majors. The good news is that there are very few philosophy majors wandering aimlessly among the unemployed and homeless.

I have argued long that logic could be taught effectively at the high school level. Currently we offer courses identified as *History of Ideas* and *Great Books*. I think we could easily offer one course in aesthetics as an overview of fine arts and the appreciation thereof. Metaphysics and epistemology may be beyond the critical-thinking skills of most students without extensive reading within the field. Some areas of metaphysical and ethical discussion can be theological and could be objectionable to some parents and difficult to teach objectively in a high school environment.

Someone once said that you cannot teach young women and men how to be ladies and gentlemen. Rather you teach them everything good and beautiful, and they will become ladies and gentlemen.

The value of philosophy is not as a requisite for career or professional opportunity. At a time when America is deficient in the graduation of students skilled in math and science, I would be hesitant to suggest that we need a generation of philosophers. One of my philosophy professors even suggested that we should read *about* Aristotle, and should spend very little time reading the works of Aristotle. I would suggest that we must train our youth to compete in the world community in fields of engineering, technology, manufacturing, science, genetics, and medicine with professionals who are skilled in these pragmatic fields. We also need lovers of wisdom—who would seek to understand and explain the principles of existence and reality; who would calmly and rationally react to events, especially adversity; who would deeply consider human affairs and life in general.

46

Tambourine Theology

I think there are several ways to find Christianity. You could be struck blind or dumb in a divine display of uncommon phenomena, resulting in an epiphany. This could happen on the road to Damascus en route to persecute Christians, or late one evening after four drinks, a pack of cigarettes, and a failed sexual flirtation. Gut-rending conversion has some emotional advantages over the fetal infusion of six generations of fundamentalism.

My Methodist patriarchy of Peach Hollow and my Church of Christ ancestry in Boston and Leiper's Fork are convincing arguments for predestination. Salvation would come to me either at birth or at an arbitrary age of accountability somewhere around the fifth grade or puberty, depending on my preference for immersion or alternative ritual of compliance. Any thought of *not* being a Christian in Boston or in Peach Hollow never found utterance or detection.

My steeple of choice was determined by the tragic death of my father four months before I was born. I can still hear the voice of my Uncle Allen as he led the singing with no aid from *unscriptural* instruments of music. As I have grown older and listened to the fragile voices of an aging *a cappella*, and the full orchestral splendor of contemporary Christianity, I have found a love for quietude and a longing for a time without amplification and choreography.

As the age of tambourine theology came to define the style of denominationally-diverse worship, I eventually found the Christianity of my youth in a mid-sized Church of Christ with traditionally trained voices and familiar hymnals. Within its walls I was allowed to teach Sunday school, and was fortunate to learn from wise and eloquent ministers.

As I have visited the many churches in Williamson County and Nashville, I have improved my tolerance for contemporary Christian music. I found that I understand the necessity of music for church growth. I respect the individual and group talent of singers and musicians, or a choir. I am encouraged by physical and visual exuberance of spirit-driven praise and worship. And I still feel no compulsion to participate or enjoy it.

Though I still have never entertained the demons of disbelief, nor been seduced by secular alternatives, I share the disenchantment that has come to those of us who feel the burden of organized orthodoxy, sectarian politics, and overzealous evangelicalism. When I tell fellow Christians that the hour or two in a church on a Sunday morning is probably the least spiritual moment of my week, they shriek in horror, and offer prayers of deliverance from my depravity. I have given up on trying to explain the unspeakable pleasures and importance of the demeanor, compassion, and tranquility of rational theology. A theology without the brass and percussion, without the professional sound and lighting.

I am constantly cautious and reluctant in a world of political correctness to audibly speak the words "tambourine theology." I am accused of being old. I am accused of being trapped in my fundamentally narrow doctrinal rejection of instrumental music. I even get whispered accusations ranging from liberal, secularist, humanist, to agnostic. So far, only one preacher has spoken the word atheist, but that is another issue that is more about politics than about theology and musical taste.

I think my problem with praise and worship is that I tend to prefer Sarah McLachlan, Bette Midler, Sarah Brightman, and the instrumental genius of the Eagles' "Seven Bridges Road" and the Beatles' "Norwegian Wood." I want to believe this is only a matter of taste and not indicative of a slippery slope of secularism.

The irony of it all is that, having been in different churches on Sunday mornings, I have found beneath the veneer of entertainment an amazing depth of love and fellowship, bonded secularly by faith and reason. I have found a greater wonder of and devotion to Christianity, and I don't get bruises on my thigh or on the heel of my left hand.

47

THE CORRUPTION OF CHILDREN

In one of the closing scenes of the movie version of *Inherit the Wind*, Spencer Tracy, in the role of Clarence Darrow, quotes from Proverbs 11:29—"He that troubleth his own house..."—just before he puts copies of the *Holy Bible* and *On the Origin of Species* into his briefcase. I have watched this on late-night satellite television until it is archived forever in my brain beside *To Kill a Mockingbird*.

Those of you who arrived late to the South may have missed our regional reluctance to racial understanding and academic honesty within the walls of rural public education and fundamentalist Sunday school. The story of John Scopes and the Dayton, Tennessee, trial, jokingly referred to as the Monkey Trial, was documented on front pages of newspapers, North and South. Scopes was found guilty and fined a minimal sum for violating a state law that prohibited teaching evolution in public schools.

The trial began as a tourist phenomenon to draw a crowd to the public square and Main Street of Dayton. It became much more. Fundamentalist rural Tennessee and the liberal Eastern media created a comedic but historic spectacle involving William Jennings Bryan and Clarence Darrow.

In recent days, I have been reading again the writings of

Plato, including *Apology*, in which Socrates defends his conduct as a philosopher. Charges within the evidence presented against him include corrupting the youth of Athens, and denial of the gods.

The difference in importance between Scopes and Socrates is obvious. The similarities often go unnoticed. Teachers or philosophers who encourage students to think critically, contemplate the complexity of the universe, or question paradigms, are sometimes chastised by public consensus. Great men of science and thinkers of periods of enlightenment have found themselves in conflict with public opinion and religious orthodoxy. From Socrates to Jesus to Copernicus to Galileo to Darwin, those who challenged the existing order were accused of corrupting the youth and denying existing iconic deities. Through the history of the Reformation, the Civil Rights Movement, advanced scientific and medical research, and innovation in education, persons often defamed the images of conservatism and Christianity, with their opposition to human liberty and intellectual freedom.

More recently, talk-radio personalities publicly assail classroom assignments in schools, and challenge the academic diversity of public education. Parents, in opposing assigned readings that they find offensive, often would deny access to other students for reasons of ideology. Legislators would ban or disclaim the content of some chapters in our science textbooks

There is, however, the risk that those of us who are advocates of secular intellectual freedom may at times become intolerant of religious expression. With caution, we avoid sectarian instruction in the classroom. The proper guidelines seem to be: the protection of all individual religious freedom, and the non-participatory role of government in matters of collective religion. Those of us in elected public office, who hold positions of authority in public education, are prohibited by law and logic from imposing our religious views on our youth or challenging their religious beliefs, writings, symbols, or practices.

Those of us who find an attraction to philosophy and the Socratic method of reasoning, often derive delight from circuitously challenging the advocates of certainty. We thrive on the gamesmanship of challenging the Sophists in the Greek marketplace who define truth and virtue in their own street-vendor rhetoric. We love confounding the Pharisees in the Temple courtyard in Jerusalem. We applaud Luther as he rattled the ramparts of royal and papal Christendom.

I wish that I could trace their steps, sharing their courage and mischief, into the churches, temples, mosques, courtrooms, classrooms, and halls of government, and identify with those thinkers and reformers who have advanced human thought and liberty. We live in a time and place in which the Sophists and Pharisees have changed their raiment and taken new names, and sit in seats of authority, and we would be at risk if they thought we were corrupting their youth or questioning their gods.

48

The Handiwork of God

One of the historical greats in the world of science, in frustration, referred to a function of science that he could not explain, as the handiwork of God. As scientists come to explain the complexity of the universe with more certainty, they tend to assign less attribution to God. In some harmony of faith and reason, we look to God for explanations of infinity, eternity, and other inexplicable attributes, beyond the Father image of Mosaic literature and the apostolic writings.

Descartes wrote in *Meditations on First Philosophy*, "I have always thought that two issues—namely, God and the soul—are chief among those that ought to be demonstrated with the aid of philosophy rather than theology."

The question is, at what point of comprehensibility do the accepted principles of science cease to be the handiwork of God? Agriculture, medicine, industry, and other fields of endeavor have become predictable, based on experience and accepted principles of logic. Routine and repetition should make them no less the handiwork of God.

I don't understand the epistemological line between theology and philosophy. The obvious difference is the verbiage of the practitioners of each field of study. When we think of theology, we often think of preachers. This has some validity.

If you only hear the Sunday morning pulpit messages in most churches, you miss the greater dimension of theology. In my religious search, I have come to know and converse with many preachers who truly are theologians. These are educated men, in Holy Scripture and classical philosophical literature. In contemporary religious pulpits, philosophy can be threatening to faith. Theologians must become preachers and pastors on Sunday mornings. Sunday school, and other periods of religious scholarship, provide some open dialogue with members who seek the curiosity of theology.

In traditional Southern religion, we believe that God exists because it is written in the Bible, and we believe the Bible because it is the Word of God. This suffices for traditional Southern believers. Traditional Southern religion has not been very tolerant of philosophical dialogue. Inquiring minds have: 1) continued to go to church because it made Mama happy; 2) left the church seeking something deeper; 3) pursued philosophical logic and followed their hearts into a deeper faith within the church.

Traditional Southern religion may have missed much of the metaphorical beauty of the Bible in its insistence on literal biblical interpretation. We nodded in silent consent while discussing the physical dimensions of Heaven, or the painful horror of Hell. We spoke literally of streets of gold and gates of pearl. We espoused a creation completed in 144 hours, or six days. Many of my generation left the churches of literal fundamentalism.

As I visit churches on Sunday morning, I listen to the pulpit message and comments from individuals. I am hearing a generation that is very happy with the church they have found, believing in the Messianic nature of Jesus, and a God that has pre-knowledge and continuing control of the changing configuration of the universe and the future of human conduct.

Religion is a comforter. Faith is a refuge from intellectual uncertainty and scientific curiosity.

One should not try to separate theology from philosophy and the physical sciences. Knowledge of God, whether derived from scriptural revelation or from empiricism or rationalism, fits into the greater body of truth. The totality of truth is not contained within one document, but preceded the creation. Truth predates and transcends Hebrew, Greek, and Latin.

None, or at least few, of us would question the spiritual presence within God's earthly kingdom. Religion, as conceived in the mind of God, exists as an absolute for purposes known only to the mind of God. I don't know if time spent on Earth is an impediment to ultimate spiritual life, or if we are the temporal custodians of spirituality. Whichever be true, we are given logic to find a purpose, and ethics to make it happen. Some of God's handiwork I still can't explain, but accept it as such.

49

God's Will, Sunday Morning

The conflict between twenty-seven consecutive weeks of perfect church attendance and a nineteen-year tradition of attending every hour of the Southern Festival of Books in Nashville bothered me to some degree as the Sunday in conflict approached. Within the tradition of my earlier religious tradition, choosing a book festival over Sunday morning worship was akin to sacrilege, or blasphemy.

My attendance at the Southern Festival began around 1990. I had the good fortune of being introduced as a philosopher and playwright, and I was hooked on the dream of being either or both. Only a death within the immediate family has kept me away, and then only the final Sunday of one festival.

Normally, I would not let church interfere with a book festival. However, I had begun a sequence of visiting a different church every Sunday and had done so for six months. Many of my friends talk to God regularly for counsel in matters of conflict such as this. Some would see this as a conflict between the spiritual and the secular. Spiritual people would hear God insist that church attendance was first priority. Secular people would more likely hear God favor the learning experience of a book-related event.

Politics, Preaching & Philosophy

Until my late thirties, most of my Sunday mornings revolved around Sunday school, most of that time as the teacher. It is difficult to explain my intermittent estrangement from formal religion. Part of it came from experiences during the Vietnam War resistance and the Civil Rights Movement. The two most compelling moral issues in my world were not shared by most members of my congregation. I listened to Sunday morning prayers for a military victory. I listened to the concerns of our membership facing the menace of racial integration within the pews of Southern Christianity.

I endured through this difficult time. Our congregation became more and more conservative and more and more Republican, and I hid my liberal philosophy within the teaching of Jesus, and few people realized it was liberal.

My attraction to Christianity had two sources—a spiritual pathos for humanity and an academic system of ethics and morals. I found both of these to be compatible with my theology. I also found a troubling contradiction. The church seemed to turn inward and limit its compassion and tolerance to its membership. I watched churches become Sunday morning enclaves of religious intolerance. Secondly, I watched Sunday mornings become more doctrine and ritual with definitions of ethics and morals more consistent with Southern tradition than a more universal empathy and harmony with humankind.

I don't know if I went left, or got left. I couldn't find the Christianity of my childhood. Many of us who sought liberal Christianity found an intellectual incompleteness inside the church, and a countervailing spiritual incompleteness outside the church. The conflict of faith and reason, the conflict of formal and personal worship, the conflict of Southern culture and New Testament Christianity, created for me a paradox in which my Sunday morning in church was the lowest spiritual and intellectual hour of my week.

In Southern culture, many consider church affiliation as imperative. Church attendance is seen as a requisite for social respectability. My avowed insistence that I am a member of the Church of Christ evokes quizzical looks of disbelief and distrust. Among liberals and intellectuals, I feel the painful image of our past bigotry and doctrinal intolerance. Among fellow Church of Christ members, I feel their rejection and distrust of liberal Christianity. In the quiet of my bedroom, or the starlit sanctity of my patio, I find a tolerant and loving God. I find a more spiritual environment than I find in the brick and mortar of church.

As I mingle among the many on Sunday morning, I talk to people who fill charismatic and evangelical churches with thousands of members. I talk to others who cling to the past and fragile future of small, rural congregations. I talk to some people who feel closer to God at book festivals.

50

Pastors, Preachers, and Philosophers

Every July, our church held a revival, or protracted meeting, beginning on Sunday and ending the following Sunday might. The purpose was primarily to save the lost, and beg God's forgiveness for the sins of the faithful. Those of you who did not grow up in rural fundamentalism may find this lacking in logic.

In the summer of 1948, four days before my twelfth birthday, I was baptized for the remission of sins in the swimming hole in a creek that ran beside the church building. We, the pre-teen children of the faithful, discussed among ourselves and our parents the question of when one reaches the age of accountability. With baptism came membership in two churches—the congregation of Christians that met at Boston, Tennessee, and the Church of Christ as defined and chronicled in the New Testament. Also, for me, I became scripturally eligible to teach Sunday school, a career upon which I embarked the following Sunday.

During my freshman year at Lipscomb University, on two occasions I substituted for another Lipscomb student who was the regular preacher for another small congregation. Preaching for a small congregation of the Church of Christ required little theological depth. My knowledge of the King James Bible and the simplicity of our plan of salvation gave me sufficient skills for which I was paid two dollars each Sunday.

I envy the charismatic speakers who can draw thousands on Sunday mornings and attract long lines at bookstores, signing books for admiring fans who drive across state lines to purchase their printed words and reach out to touch these men of God. I watch these spiritual giants on television and scan the pages of their books, and ask, Why? How have we become attracted to pop-culture pulpits with feel-good motivational speeches delivered with the skill of a tent-revivalist with no apparent intellectual awareness of the complexity of theology?

I admire, but may not envy, local ministers who, with intense labor, provide the pastoral love for their congregations and the broader community. Pastors take the lead in visiting the fatherless and the widows. They are at bedside and graveside, and share the congregational suffering and sorrow. As we say jokingly, they deliver words that comfort the afflicted and afflict the comfortable. They share the message of God's grace and forgiveness, and chastise the flock for moral indiscretions and sins of omission. Churches, and their hardworking pastors, have been and continue to be the sustaining storehouse of benevolence and moral stability of their communities.

When I attend the Sunday morning periods of praise and worship, with music and responsive readings, I come away hungry. I love the fellowship of the many congregations I have visited, including the fundamentalism of southern Williamson County and two congregations of Unitarian liberals.

Many years ago, when I set out in search of academic challenges, I found among my fellow Christians a fear of philosophy. I was surrounded by elders and church leaders who were skeptical of the thoughts and writings of the intellectual giants of Western Philosophy.

Politics, Preaching & Philosophy

When I sit in the pews of major denominations and nondenominational community churches, I talk to church members who feel good about their pastor and style of praise and worship. They have found a home congregation, usually after some searching and separation from a previous affiliation. The works of compassion and benevolence by the staff and ministry are the foundation of the church community. These pastors are also the custodians of biblical literalism and cultural morality as they deliver the stories of Old Testament heroes, apostolic writings, and the words of Jesus.

Occasionally, I spend some time and share a cup of coffee with these men and women of faith who are also philosophers and theologians, who find time within their calling as preacher or pastor to share with me a quote from Descartes, Hume, or Leibniz in our search for the ultimate splendor and logical certainty of God.

51

THE GOD OF POLITICS

Persons who have found a steeple of preference are blessed in having a personal pastor. In my recent spiritual odyssey, I have been blessed in sharing time with many men and women of faith. In not having only one pastor, I feel much more blessed in having found shepherding ministers in Presbyterian, Episcopalian, Unitarian, and nondenominational churches who have touched my life. Through this interaction, I may have influenced some Sunday morning sermons, hopefully for the better, and I have been able to learn from them outside the constriction of the pulpit and oppression of orthodoxy.

In a meeting over coffee, one of them told me a story of a minister confronted by a person who strongly avowed, "I do not believe in your God." After which the minister asked his antagonist to tell him about the God in which he did not believe. The supposed non-theist then described in detail some theology that contained fragments of mythology, superstition, and fundamentalist literalism, framed in a contemporary pop-culture anthropomorphic image of a personal deity who bore no similarity to the God of a rational theologian.

We of the Christian faith worship the God of the Old and New Testaments of our Bible. We use the names Jehovah or Yahweh or the simple English designation, God. Monotheism, obviously, can only have one God. Monotheists who believe in a god with a different name, whose message comes from a different prophet, whose followers worship differently, are often thought to be, or referred to, as infidels. Most of my friends are monotheists, believing in one God, but I respect the several nonbelievers within the boundaries of my corner of humanity

Some historians, anthropologists, and philosophers have argued that man created God, rather than God creating man. I believe that man may have misinterpreted God; therefore, he sees God in his own image rather than God's biblical image.

Having grown up in a fundamentalist environment, I believed in the revealed God, not so much a personal God. He was the God of the Jews, the Creator, the Christian God. He had capacities that we define in human terminology—knowing, seeing, speaking, loving, touching, rebuking, and forgiving. He was also the God of nature. He was the author of beneficent conduct and moral restraint. He was the judge of ethics and morals.

Today, as I intermingle with Christians of many stripes, I hear people speak of God very differently from the God of my youth. Most recently, I was concerned by those who had sought the intervention of God in the secular function of the democratic elective process. I read newspaper accounts of pastors and politicians, at political gatherings, who had prayed that God would bring to the presidency a man of faith who shares our values, who would fight for us, who would be there for us as a force for good.

The irony of this is that, particularly in Williamson County, as in much of the South, the Republican Party is dominated by social conservatives. According to newspaper accounts, most of the prayers during the election had come from Republicans. In prayer, we ask for a person who is wise, who is fair, who represents family values, who believes in God, who loves America, who is compassionate, who is a peacemaker. Moral decorum and the IRS dictate that Christians not name candidates or parties in their prayers. This is equally true for Democrats and Republicans.

Did God in fact hear the generic prayers of the Republican supplication and impose His judgment over their preference? Did the fervent prayers of Democrats, less public, less vocal, touch the heart of God with greater poignancy than the prayers of Republicans? Did God turn a deaf ear to America, as a minor player in the community of nations, and leave us to our own vices? Did we, as a secular nation, choose a President by the process of electoral votes derived from the majority will of the several states?

52

Tolerance, Condescension, and Understanding

There may be the perception that the majority-thought of conservative and Republican Williamson County is an immovable, inflexible tradition that no intensity of argumentation can change. As a Liberal and Democrat, I struggle trying to defend and promote minority opinions in almost all political, religious, and philosophical exchanges. This continuing dialogue could have the potential for bilateral intolerance. Within this standoff, we often accuse each other of intolerance, and in so doing, we appear to be equally intolerant.

The second error of this discussion is the assumption that the word *tolerance* is the opposite of the word *intolerance*. One of the more important principles of textbook philosophy is that some realities do not have opposites, but rather require a word that implies an absence of the other.

We also err in the assumption that tolerance and intolerance are attributes available only to the majority. The image of majority intolerance is perpetuated by disproportionate power—legislative, administrative, or social. Those who are continually within the minority eventually develop the victim syndrome. Tolerance within the minority camp is often interpreted as submission or appeasement.

If or when the majority-thought takes on an assumption of being beyond dispute and undeniable, tolerance takes on the appearance of condescension. While we see tolerance as coming from virtue-based humility, condescension implies lowering oneself in some concession that suggests lesser importance of the opposing thought, and becomes demeaning. Majority condescension is usually arrogant. Minority condescension is more often elitist.

Condescension is a dubious display of tolerance, which becomes offensively intolerant. We can usually categorize condescension as an affectation coming from a false humility.

We need to find a better word for tolerance. Tolerance carries the connotation of putting up with something that is irritating or unpleasant. Instead, it should entail acceptance of the validity of a differing view held by other people. I had this discussion with a respected member of the Baptist clergy who suggested the word *understanding*. Understanding does not need the support of a position of advantage. Understanding suggests an intellectual awareness of another's opinion, and respect for the historical and biographical background of an adversary holding a counter-argument. Understanding is an imperative in rational dialogue. Tolerance has a tendency to suggest an inequity in dialogue.

A few days ago I had a conversation with a woman who avowed that she was a Catholic and a Conservative. She did so after I told her of an incident in which I had tried to defend my public image as a Liberal. These admissions followed a conversation on a subject about which we completely agreed on every point. Our conversation had no opening or purpose for any thought or expression of tolerance. However, only our self-inflicted labels could have been a barrier of intolerance.

I have often argued that any statement beginning with the phrase *I believe* or *I think* is irrefutable. An antagonist might question the truth of the postulate, but the personal affirmation of belief is fact. If one says "I am a Democrat" or "I am a Republican," there is no argument. Saying "I am a Catholic" or "I am a Protestant" carries the same sanctity of being fact, not opinion. Affiliation (or membership) invites no refutation.

Why, then, do we argue? An opinion expressed as if it were fact, should be questioned and challenged for validation. Two conflicting postulates or theses, neither of which having attained the level of truth, should be identified as only postulates or theses. Such identification may not suggest untruth or falsehood.

I spend way too much of my time thinking about religion and politics. Much of this time is consumed in refining my writing skills to offer logical assumptions with or without conclusion. If the study of philosophy has any value, it is that it does not explore what we know; it explores what we believe and what we think. For me to speak of tolerance for a political view, or a sectarian ideology, or philosophical thesis, is no valid measure of its value or verity. I believe understanding is a better word than tolerance, I think.

Printed in the United States
217107BV00002B/1/P